Dear Queen

To: Deb,

Wear YOUR Crown!

Blessings,

ALSO BY DR. EDDIE CONNOR

Purposefully Prepared to Persevere

Collections of Reflections,
Volumes 1-3: Symphonies of Strength

E.CON the ICON: from Pop Culture to
President Barack Obama

Unwrap The Gift In You

Heal Your Heart

My Brother's Keeper

Dear
Queen

Jewels of Wisdom
for Loving Yourself
and Knowing Your Worth

Dr. Eddie Connor

norbrook
publishing

Also available as an ebook from Norbrook Publishing.

Library of Congress Cataloging-in-Publication Data is available upon
request.

ISBN 978-0-9970504-4-8
eBook ISBN 978-0-9970504-5-5

PRINTED IN THE UNITED STATES OF AMERICA

10 9 8 7 6 5 4 3 2 1

First Edition

To every Queen who keeps God first, leads with love, and pursues each day with purpose. You were placed on this earth because you have value, significance, and worth.

I'm here today because of the encouragement, prayers, and support from Queens like you that empowered me through tough times.

The love in you, is greater than any label that the world places on you. Believe greater, build stronger, and breakthrough farther past life's limitations.

You are a Queen. Wear your crown, embrace your royalty, love yourself, and know your worth.

"A nation can rise no higher than its women."

CONTENTS

Introduction   1

1. Know Your Worth   12

2. Fools Gold   32

3. Waiting to Exhale   43

4. What's Love Got to Do with It?   57

5. Heal Before You Deal   75

6. Red Box, Gold Bow   90

7. Break the Cycle   100

8. Focus On Your Focus   118

9. My Sister's Keeper   129

10. Build Your Queendom   162

11. Wear Your Crown   193

The Queen Code   255

Dear Queen   257

Acknowledgments   261

About the Author   262

Dear Queen

INTRODUCTION

You may have never been called "Queen," when you were growing up. Maybe no one ever saw your true gifts, magnanimity, and royalty. Yes, they admired your assets, but failed to realize you are an asset. They may have complimented your frame and figure, but didn't realize that what you possess is deeper than your sultry sun-kissed skin. Don't let that stop you, from recognizing your value.

So many times, we seek validation from what we possess and the recognition from others to solidify our value. If you don't know who you are, people will make you believe what you're not. You can never truly know WHO you are, until you know WHOSE you are. Realize and recognize that you are a Queen. You are God's chosen vessel, for such a time as this to empower and impact the world.

It's not by coincidence, that you are reading this book. Some people like to say the stars aligned. I would like to believe, the Creator of the universe who aligned the stars, had a purpose in mind for you to shine. This particular time is uniquely designed, for you to invest in yourself and know your worth on a greater level. As you know, "It's levels to this" and *Dear Queen* is the book designed with a purpose in mind, to stretch your faith and propel you to the next level.

This is your prime time, to put your life under the magnifying lens and see the royal greatness that God sees in you. When you look deep within, you will realize that God sees your royal Queen quality. He sees it, when others are blind to it. This is the time for you to recognize your value and worth.

A real Queen never has to give her body away, in exchange for love. When you are a person of love, it emanates from your total being. When you are someone who loves themselves and knows their worth, you can set the standard and expect respect in return. If someone is not willing to show you respect or wait, then they are not the one for you. Plain and simple. You can't expect to be treated right, by someone who only intends to trick you. Real love isn't selfish, it's selfless. It doesn't come to take, but to give.

Too many people, would rather be accepted than respected. They seek popularity in exchange for principles. Even to the degree, where they search for love in "likes" on social media, behave provocatively, and undress themselves for the world to see. All because they are in search of something tangible, to become a bandaid for the real love they are in search of discovering. Don't become thirsty to show off your body and trade your self-respect for attention. You are a Queen, you don't have to do that. I don't care what everybody else is doing. You're not everybody else. Maintain your royalty and dignity.

Growing up, I didn't always understand my value and worth. The idea of guys showing love or being loving, was seen as "soft." Too often as men, we are taught to play a "tough role," until we adopt a pseudo persona and can't distinguish the real from the fake. Ultimately, the fake role that we play, ends up playing us. Simply because we turn our back on those who celebrate and love us, by seeking acceptance from those who only tolerate us. In essence, we ignore those who adore us and we adore those who ignore us.

Far too often we perpetuate a Superman Syndrome, to where we wear an "S" on our chest. Yet the "S" doesn't always mean we're strong. Oftentimes, it means we're sensitive and struggling, afraid of being hurt. Real men lead with love, rather than operate as immature grown

4

boys. Love and fear cannot coexist in the same space. One will cancel out the other.

Society rarely places vulnerability and masculinity, in the same category. We differentiate the two, to only see it as femininity. My father never showed me how to love a woman, by the example he set in the household through his relationship with my mother. Fortunately there was no physical abuse, but the verbal aggression and angst hit as hard as a punch would. There were many issues which produced a chasm in the marriage, leading to a family breakdown and divorce.

I'm grateful that my mother's love, sustained me through tough times. Yet, still my young eyes internalized the frustration of a father, who failed to express love to his son. Maybe it wasn't expressed to him, when he was raised. For whatever reason, it became a burden in my teenage years, during my ordeal to battle and overcome stage four cancer.

I must say that I believe the stress, divorce, and mental discombobulation, became psychosomatic contributors to my illness. Stressors, mental health, and physical well-being are all interconnected to one's longevity of life.

In high school, I can admit that I was never the sports jock, prom king, or popular guy. I was never voted "class handsome" or "most likely to succeed." In many cases I was the least likely, because of the circumstances I faced. However, I have learned that the least likely can do the most mighty.

Oftentimes, the girls I liked, overlooked me and the ones I would have considered "high school sweethearts" had eyes for other guys. For many years I was a shy kid. Some may have called me nerdy, because I had good grades. Yet, I was always able to balance academics and athletics. I love sports and played basketball in high school, prior to my illness. You couldn't have told me that I wasn't the second coming of Michael "Air" Jordan. I think one too many "air" balls ended that dream quickly though.

I was always searching, for what is that special talent that I possessed. I found it through writing and my words became the slam dunk. Writing helped me to express my feelings, convey my thoughts, and put my pain on paper. I soon found that I could speak, as well as I could write and people began to pay attention. So I began to write love letters to ladies. I would anonymously slide a letter into a girls locker or have a friend place it in their hand.

For a long time, I was too shy to approach girls, being afraid of rejection or being "put on blast." Nothing is worse than being in school and a girl giving you three snaps and a neck roll. Only to put her hand in your face, smack her lips and say, "Boy I don't like you." I thought letters were a far better way to approach a love interest, without the pain of embarrassment or rejection.

In my English class, to my surprise, I discovered that many of my classmates genuinely enjoyed my writing and poetry. One assignment led to another and I wound up negotiating a fee to charge guys, for writing love letters to their lady friends. They could use and rewrite my words at their discretion, as long as they gave me the money upfront.

Yes, I was a bookworm, but I was also a businessman in the making. I knew the value of my words because they were forged through love, pain, isolation, and rejection. At one point, the word got around and some of the ladies found out, that it was my writing and were amazed. However, some never knew it was me. Honestly, I didn't mind the anonymity. My desire was not to be known or celebrated. The thrill was in the reaction, embrace, and love that each young lady felt from my words. I never had a chance to hold their hand or hug them, but the words from my love letter did that for me.

So, after being introspective, I decided to embrace the challenge, of writing my seventh book. I figured if I could write letters to ladies anonymously and let them know how lovely they are, then surely I could write a book that empowers Queens to know their value and how significant they are.

My aim is that *Dear* Queen, will serve as that same experience but on a deeper, transparent, inspirational, and transformative level. As you read this book, you will know your value greater, love yourself deeper, and be inspired to create substantive change.

I wrote *Dear Queen* because essentially it's a love letter in book form, to celebrate your value. I define the word "QUEEN" as **Q**uintessentially **U**nique **E**mpowering **E**veryone **N**aturally. I trust that this book will empower you to embrace your God-given gifts, see your value for what it's worth, love yourself beyond life's limitations, and

9

wear your crown. It's your time to be the Queen, that you were created to be. As you read *Dear Queen*, you will discover jewels of wisdom. These jewels will transform your thinking to love yourself, know your worth, and unlock the door to your royal identity.

You, yes YOU are priceless. Know your worth. Appreciate who you are. Embrace your gifts. Live with purpose, love yourself, and reveal your greatness within!

Reach out and let me know, how this book has empowered you. I often say, "The revolution will not be televised, it will be online and I don't want you to miss it." Please log on and connect with me, at EddieConnor.com, join me there for more information and inspiration.

Real Kings empower Queens. Link with me on social media for more royal inspiration and insight on Facebook, Instagram, and Twitter: **@EddieConnorJr**. In addition, be sure to take a selfie with your book. Post it on any of the social media sites, and use the hashtag #DearQueen. So, without further ado, let's start the journey. May you discover greater life, liberty, and love on every page, as a manual to succeed on life's stage.

CHAPTER 1

Know Your Worth

You are not on sale, don't let anybody discount you.

A few years ago, I spoke at a Women's Empowerment Symposium, along with notable speaker, Iyanla Vanzant. The central theme of our conversation, centered around discovering your inner beauty, loving yourself, and knowing your worth. Those three components are essential factors, to giving birth to your purpose and attracting the right people on your road to destiny.

What are you investing your time, energy, and resources into? Get to the place to where you understand, that it's not about what you have on the outside, but it's who you are on the inside that makes the difference.

Dear Queen, I want you to understand how beautiful, precious and significant you are. God created you in a unique way, because you are extraordinarily special. You are divinely designed with a purpose in mind. So many people judge you, but don't know you. They don't know the struggles that you have endured and the strength you exercised to overcome it.

Oftentimes we as men do you a disservice, by only taking you for face value. We admire your outer frame, more than your focus and aim. We look at the outer appearance more than your inner value and self-worth. We live in a hypersexual society that places more emphasis on someone's body than their mind, soul, and spirit. Never trade self-respect, for a desire to receive attention.

LIKES DON'T EQUAL LOVE

You are not a Facebook or Instagram post, stop waiting on

people to "like" you and start loving yourself. Too often we waste time, by looking for somebody to love us. When you realize that your love is worth looking for, then you'll stop looking for someone to love you. When you start becoming a person of love, you will begin receiving love in a greater way. If love for self doesn't begin within, everything else is meaningless. Begin to nurture your value and inner wealth. You're not truly wealthy, until you have something that money can't buy. If you are bankrupt on the inside, you will soon be bankrupt on the outside.

Realize that you are not on sale, so don't let anybody discount your value. You're too priceless, to be on a clearance rack. Know your worth. Never reduce yourself to fit in with people, who don't like you anyway. Your presence is a present, be careful who you give it to. Why minimize and make yourself small, at the expense of seeking acceptance from others? Your value isn't tied to WHAT people think

14

about you. It's HOW you think about yourself. Don't let the opinions of others, interrupt the true thoughts of who you are. Value you!

If they can't appreciate you now, they sure won't be able to embrace you in the future. You may have been stepped on, talked about, betrayed, bruised, abused, left for dead, or forsaken but you still have value!

Despite what's been done to you, it can't erase the value that's inside of you. When you stop living your life to please people and start pleasing God, then everything else will fall into place. Make up your mind, to be everything that God created you to be in every way, everyday.

ASSET OR LIABILITY?

People are assets or liabilities. They either add to your value or subtract from it. If they're not adding, then subtract them from your life. God only brings people into your life, to do two things: add and multiply. If people bring division to your life, to divide you from your destiny and subtract your substance, then it's time to do some personal inventory. When you really know your self-worth, you surround yourself with people who enhance it, not diminish it.

Your value doesn't diminish, because someone failed to recognize it. Don't lose your value, because someone lost sight of who you are. Never beg a man to see the value in you Queen. If he doesn't see it, that means he wasn't given the eyes for it. The right King will see your true value and acknowledge it.

You can't truly love, respect, and value somebody else until you love, respect, and value yourself. It's not about what you have, it's about who you are that is significant. Nothing you own on the outside, comes close to the value that you have on the inside.

SELF-ESTEEM

Former First Lady of the United States, Eleanor Roosevelt declared, "No one can make you feel inferior, without your consent." Stop giving people permission to trespass on your emotions. It's called "self-esteem" for a reason, because the value of self begins with you. It's not based on other people's feelings of you. Oftentimes, the way we feel about ourselves is directly impacted, by how others have treated or mistreated us. Inadequate love from others, leads to a lack of love for self.

How do I love myself, if no one expressed loved to me? This is a question that many people grapple with internally. However, it begins with forgiving those who have mistreated you and appropriating God's love, so that you understand your life has value. You can't live an abundant life mentally trapped in sadness, sickness, and thoughts of suicide. You have to heal from the hurt and pain, that you have experienced, in order to free yourself from the vestiges of your past.

TAKE OFF THE MASK

Putting on a fancy dress, heels, and makeup won't matter, if your mind isn't made up to see your self-worth. Oftentimes we are dressed up on the outside, but messed up on the inside. Some people perfume their pain. They mask it with makeup. They spray it with Givenchy, but still feel ugly internally.

It won't matter how much someone tells you how beautiful you are, if you don't see beauty in yourself. Someone telling you how much they love you, won't matter until you begin to love yourself. I hope my words become like a loving hand that lifts your chin, looks you in the eyes, and speaks life into the Queen that's inside of you.

It's not your fault that someone decided to take advantage of your heart, mind, and body when you were vulnerable. The ones we entrusted, entrapped and introduced us to horrific pain. They were supposed to use their hands to heal and help you, but they hurt and harmed you by stealing your innocence. You know that you are in the hands of a manipulator, when you end up feeling guilty for what they did to you. If they are hurting you, that's not love. Verbal and physical abuse is not love. Stop blaming yourself and begin the healing process of loving yourself. You are not a victim. You are victorious.

Despite being abused, God can still use you. God had His hand on you before the enemy attacked you, which means there is a plan for your life. God hears every one of your silent screams and cries. Even now, He is turning your pain into power and tears into joy. He can create peace from your broken pieces.

So many times we hide behind a mask, to conceal the past. Take off the mask and begin to look within, the mirror of your soul. Many times we are afraid to address issues within, because it brings up old memories, scars, and hurt. How can you heal from it, if you won't deal with it? Stop going through life numb and on auto-pilot. Take control of your life, get in the drivers seat and press forward on the road to your destiny.

Love, tranquility, and hope does not come from the external, it begins internally. It all begins from within. The outside won't fix the inside, until you deal with what is on the inside first. When you work on yourself from within, the true beauty of you will shine through. Take off the mask to reveal the mess and misery, that only God can remedy. Don't give up and die inside. You can live through dying places and share a great testimony, as a result of it. Trust God to heal it, when you take off the mask to reveal it.

WHO BETTER THAN YOU?

Sometime ago, I ran into a young lady that I was interested

in dating. While we were talking she said, "I need to apologize to you, because I messed things up by being insecure." I reminded the young lady, that I only had eyes for her and just wanted her to see, what I saw in her at that time. She replied, "It was never about you seeing someone else. The issue was I didn't see my self-worth, which prevented me from seeing what you saw in me." It was a very transparent and powerful statement to make. How many times have you messed up potential opportunities and relationships, because you didn't think you were good enough?

When I was pursuing her, she was elusive and I never understood the reason behind it. Eventually, she told me the cause. She informed me about how she spoke to a mutual friend. She said, "I would tell them, I think Eddie can do better than me." The trusted friend would ask her, "Who is better?"

Indeed and in fact, no one is 100 percent secure in themselves. We all have personal insecurities, but it becomes an impenetrable force when we allow ourselves to get in the way of our progress. It takes growth to be secure and love yourself. There are some interpersonal places, that I am still growing in each day. Being secure in who you are is not an episodic event, it's a daily process to love yourself and know your worth. Our friend was right to ask the question, "Who better than you?" Only you can provide the right response, in your words and deeds.

YOU'RE FINE, BUT WHAT ELSE?

Beauty is only skin deep, because so many people are mentally shallow. Besides your 36-24-36 voluptuous and splendiferous physique, what else do you possess? A pretty face means nothing, if you have an ugly attitude. In essence, it just makes you ugly altogether. Your attitude and personality should be a fragrance, not an odor.

Yes, your magnanimous pulchritude can get you in the door, but only character and integrity will keep you in the building. Too often we adopt a skewed view of beauty, juxtaposed in the framework of self-worth. This often derives from a Westernized standard view, of the definitive measure for sexiness and success.

Stop comparing yourself to what you see on TV, in magazines, and the latest trends. Don't follow the trend, set the trend. Your natural beauty, is greater than cosmetic enhancements. You will drive yourself crazy trying to keep up with a celebrity, who is battling their own insecurities. Your worth isn't based on the size of your nose. Each day, you are blessed to be alive to breathe the pristine air, flowing through your lungs. In the book of Genesis, when God created the world, He spoke it into existence. However, when He created humanity, He rolled up his sleeves, put His hands in the dust of the ground and breathed life. You're

fearfully and wonderfully made. Embrace your strengths.

Who said your hair is too nappy or kinky? The only

naps and kinks, are the ones in your mind. You have a

relaxer, but you're still uptight. Lord, have mercy. The world

is clamoring for lip injections, but you let somebody tell you

that your lips are too big. You should tell them "My lips are

big enough, to open up my big mouth and thank God for

being alive." Tell them "Yes, my big lips will speak truth to

power, to defend the least, the lost, the left out, the littlest,

and the last in our society. You're not too dark or too light,

God made you just right. Let the world know, that black

don't crack and brown won't let you down.

Don't allow negative opinions and self-doubt, to

occupy your mind and detract from your true beauty. Look in

the mirror of your soul and love yourself, until the hurt is

replaced with healing. At the end of the day, what is in you, is far greater than what is on you. I know you're fine but are you worth someone's time? What are curves, without character? What is a body, if there is no brain?

WHAT'S ON THE TABLE?

What do you bring to the table? Is it substance or just a pretty smile? Victorious faith or just your voluptuous figure? Bring something to the table that the eyes can't see, so your mind can discern, as your ears are receptive. Just because they are attractive, doesn't mean that you are compatible. Learn how to hear, what people are not saying. Be more concerned about your character, than your curves. Be more focused on his wisdom, rather than what's in his wallet.

You're more than what you have, on the outside. Look within, there's a great treasure of strength and beauty on the inside. Let them see the true you, through your value. You are a blessing to somebody and if they don't recognize it, that's their loss.

VALUE YOU

See the value in yourself, appreciate who you are, and the right people will do the same. Knowing your worth truly begins from within. You have had enough people come into your life, to make withdrawals. Now is the time to make substantive deposits into your life. Make an investment in yourself, there is value within you. When you invest in yourself, you will see that your value is far greater than anything you could ever purchase.

You are worth more than money, cars, clothes, and amenities. Having a beautiful exterior with nothing in your mind, is like having a *Louis Vuitton* bag with no money inside. Your value and worth doesn't originate from the outside-in, it begins from the inside-out. Don't let anyone or anything diminish your value. You are not priced less, you are priceless!

A QUEEN'S WORTH

If you don't recognize your value, why would anybody else? You may have been crushed and stepped on, but you still have value. You're too great to be good and you're too amazing to be average. *Dear Queen*, you are a diamond, but some men prefer cubic zirconium and rhinestones.

Don't stop shining and lower your value, just to say that you have somebody. Shine on your own and the right person will shine with you. Know your worth and let your value shine through. A city set on a hill cannot be hidden. A candle ignited by a flame is meant to shine. So too are you created to be great and walk in the uniqueness of your royalty, purposefully. Don't be afraid to be amazing!

KNOW WHAT YOU WANT

If you don't know what you want, people will decide what you get. It's worth knowing your worth and it's worth knowing what you want too. A lot of people fall into one or all of the three categories below. Do any of these fit you?

1. Those who don't know what they want.

2. Those who don't get what they want.

3. Those who know what they want and when they get it, they don't want it.

1. Those who don't know what they want.

One thing you have to know, is what you want. Whether that's in a career, relationship, or simply ordering from the menu at dinner. If you're indecisive, someone will make a decision for you. The decision will generally be what you don't want, because you haven't expressed what you do want. How do you know what you don't want, if you don't know what you do want? Are you confused yet? Well, so is the person who doesn't know what they want. Avoid the confusion, by making a decision.

So you say, "Well, I just want someone to love me and treat me like a Queen." Okay, so the man showed up to do both of those things, but you didn't want him. A lot of times we are indecisive, because we fear rejection. We don't want to hurt others, but we don't want to be hurt either. So because we have been hurt, now our guard is up and we're suspicious of everybody. As you're suspicious of others, now they become suspicious of you and the cycle continues.

2. Those who don't get what they want.

You say, "Well I know what I want, but I'm not getting it." Why? What are you doing, that is preventing you from attaining it? You will continue to get what you don't want, if you keep focusing on what you don't want. I get it, you don't want to be hurt or taken for granted. However, if that's all you focus on, that's all you're going to attract. What you're attracting, is directly connected to what you're focusing on. Change your focus and you'll change, what you attract.

3. Those who know what they want and when they get it, they don't want it.

Like they say, if you're looking for an excuse you will find one. If you're looking for the imperfections in others, you will find those too. While we're looking at everyone else's imperfections, we seemingly glance over our own and remain blind to what we do. You may say, "I want somebody who is in shape, has a million dollars, big house, and a foreign car." Well, do you have any of that? What shape are you in financially, mentally, physically, and spiritually? Essentially, what are you bringing to the table, other than an appetite? If you don't know your value, what you want, or what you bring to the table, then you will find yourself on someone's menu.

CHAPTER 2

Fools Gold

Everybody plays the fool,
but the tragedy is remaining a fool.

Everything that looks good on the outside, isn't always what it portrays itself to be on the inside. You've heard the term, "Everything that glitters isn't gold." People and situations are more than what meets the eye. I once heard somebody say, "Real eyes, realize, real lies." One's real eyes, are not what's on the outside. Real eyes have discernment that is on the inside. If you have sight but no vision, then you're still blind. Sight is of the eyes, but vision derives from the heart.

There are some people who are good to you, but not any good for you. They see you with their eyes, but their heart is far from you. A person's worth in your life, should be

determined by their actions. Do they build or break you?

Do they encourage or discourage you? If they're not adding

to your life, then you need to subtract them from your life.

Don't waste your time entertaining negativity and

foolishness. Everybody plays the fool sometime, but the

tragedy is remaining a fool.

WHY DO FOOLS FALL IN LOVE?

Let's be honest, many times we know how a relationship or

situation is going to end, before it begins. However, we allow

our bodies and hearts to take us, where our minds can't keep

us. Don't fool yourself into thinking that you can change

someone, by ignoring the red flags. Begin to walk in

wisdom, so you can make the right decisions. Wisdom is

never determined by years, it's defined by experience. It's not

about your age or wage, its about your stage of maturity. You can be an old fool, but you can also be young and wise. How you respond to challenges, tells whether you are wise or foolish.

The fool is the one who continues to make the same mistake, expecting a different result. Don't let anybody cast you, for a starring role, to play the fool in your own *Lifetime* movie. Every lesson is a blessing, so learn from your mistakes.

If you keep making the same mistake, then it's no longer a mistake, it's a decision. Be more wiser, than you were foolish. Never do permanent things with temporary people, because it will leave permanent scars. The scars, bruises, and brokenness that our hearts have incurred, need healing in order to experience real love. Fools may fall in love, but they won't stay in love. Eventually, one of the two will gain wisdom and put the foolishness behind them.

My *Dear Queen*, my beautiful sister, lift up your

head, and look into the mirror of your beautiful soul. Your past may be marred in pain, but your future is bright as the sun. Never expect wisdom to flow from the lips of a fool or joker. It's only reserved for a King and Queen.

JEWEL OR JUDAS?

Your next kiss won't be from a Judas, it will be from a jewel that God will use to lift your life. A Judas will betray you with a sweet kiss, that leaves bitter scars. A jewel shares truth, love, and inspiration that heals scars to make your life better.

Pray for discernment, so that God can reveal what has been concealed. His direction is for your protection. The past may have broken your heart, but real love will give you a brand new start. Real love is more than words, its actions will transform your world. The right arms and hands won't harm or stress you. They will caress and bless you.

Don't be fooled by sleight of hand. Every hand extended is not to give, sometimes it's to take. Stop falling for people, who are not capable of catching you. Make sure they have the right hands to support, love, and strengthen you. Fall in love with someone, who is capable of catching you.

Beware! Real love doesn't step into your life to TAKE, it's on assignment to GIVE. Real love is not impressed with HOW much you have, it's focused on WHO you are. Recognize your value, love yourself through every circumstance and process, so that you can make greater progress.

IT'S ALL ADDING UP

Sometimes God adds to your life, by subtracting people from it. Let the wrong people go, to create room for the right people to walk in your life. Surround yourself with people, who will invest in your value and love you through what you go through. Trust the process, it's a setup for greater success.

ELEVATE

You can't experience NEW things, if you're doing the same OLD thing! You can't elevate your life, until you elevate your mind to think on a higher level. You're insane, if you're expecting different results, from doing the same thing. Begin to break out of your comfort zone, because comfort is the enemy of achievement.

What's ahead of you, is far greater than what you left behind. Greatness is within you. Begin to challenge yourself, set higher standards, create new goals, inspire people, think big, dream bigger, and live on a greater level.

GET OUT OF THE WAY

Get out of your own way, so that God can make a way. Never let ego, selfish pride, and arrogance impede your progress.

It's not always an outside force that inhibits your progress, sometimes it's you. Get out of the way, so that God can bless you in an unlimited way. Nobody can stop it or block it. What God has for you, is for you. Don't relinquish the goal, but go back and revisit the plan to transform it into action.

What you feed your mind today, will grow in your life tomorrow. Essentially, what you sow will grow. When your mind is positive, the darkness around you can never dim the light within you. Stop focusing and stressing about what you don't have in your possession. Take the focus off your weaknesses and deficiencies. When you are weak, that's when God will be strong for you. Change your mindset. Begin to hone in on what you do have and use it. By using what you have, it will elevate you above every setback.

BAG LADY, BROKEN BAGS

In her song *Bag Lady*, Erykah Badu sings, "Bag lady you gone hurt your back, dragging all them bags like that. I guess nobody ever told you, all you must hold onto is you." Stop carrying around bags of hurt, abuse, bitterness, and brokenness. Begin to lighten your load and rid yourself, of things that weigh you down. Yes, it's a designer bag, but the stuff that you're carrying in it, breaks you down.

Beautiful bags on the outside, but brokenness on the inside. It's like carrying an expensive *Birkin* bag, with only two pennies in it. You look good on the outside, but your value is diminished on the inside. You dress rich, but you're poor in spirit. It's like being a sharp dresser, with a dull mind. Don't get caught up in having things, to where things begin to have you. Throw the baggage in the garbage. You will be foolish to keep holding onto what hurts you. Let it go. It's crowding your space. It's crowding your thoughts of peace and tranquility. The bag of your past, is weighing down your present and future relationships. The bag of hurt is weighing down your self esteem. Let it go or you will never grow. The most important person in your life is you.

Hold on to what God gave you and placed in you. God gave

you a gift in Him and placed a gift of love in yourself. Love

the gift that He gave you, in you.

I'VE GOT THE POWER

You have power within you, that you haven't tapped into

yet. You have a rich reservoir of resilience on the inside.

Discover it and maximize every moment! To do that, you

may have to love some people from a distance. Begin to

distance yourself from people who drain you of your time,

energy, and patience. If you can't change the people that

you're around, then you must change the people that you're

around. There are some people in your life, that you must

bless and release. It may hurt to let go, but it will hurt you

more in the long run if you refuse to let go. A better you

begins by surrounding yourself, with a better crew.

Get away from the dream killers and people, who only keep you in a place of negativity. You can't elevate higher, if you're connected to negative people. Get connected to people who challenge you to be a better you. Shake yourself free from stinking thinking, toxic relationships, and dead weight that is a burden to your life. God will elevate you, in the face of those who hate you. Surround yourself with those who elevate you and bring out the best in you. It's a new day for new goals, new opportunities, and new possibilities, but you have to elevate your mind to make it your reality.

Invest in your treasure within. The treasure of your heart, soul, and destined goal. When you walk in purpose and vision, the right doors of provision will open. The right people will hold open those doors, not to fool you but to bring out greatness in you. If you're thinking junk, you will never become a jewel. How can you become wise, if you're thinking like a fool?

Below are three wise steps to take, in the face of foolishness:

1. Walk With The Wise.

You will become who you hang around. Your association will bring about assimilation. "Become wise by walking with the wise; hang out with fools and your life will fall to pieces." (Proverbs 13:20)

2. Never Debate With A Fool.

Smart people know what to say. Wise people know whether or not to say it. Never argue with a fool, it makes it hard to tell who is who.

3. Know The difference.

Walk daily with discernment. There's a difference between being different and looking foolish. Choose wisely.

CHAPTER 3

Waiting to Exhale

Waiting for what you want,
is better than settling for what you don't want.

T hey say, "All good things come to those who wait." The truth is that good things come to those, who work while they wait. One of the greatest tragedies is to breathe life, but never live it. Don't just exist, it's time to live. Every breath you take and move you make, must motivate you to aspire higher. If you can inhale and exhale, that's enough to know that you're blessed. If you have a pulse, you have a purpose.

Breathe life into every dead dream and work towards, what you've been waiting to receive. This is the season to activate your gifts within. God gave you everything that you need to win. Dig deep within the soil of your soul and create something great with your gifts.

As you seek to exhale, don't allow anything to choke your purpose. Sometimes our dreams are choked by struggle and hardship. Some of us have been choked by bad relationships, to where we have lowered our expectation. Don't allow life to apprehend your mindset, there is power within you to regain control of your life.

The situation may look insurmountable, but just inhale and exhale. Breathe and believe, that things will work out. In every situation that looks IMPOSSIBLE, is the word disguised as I'M POSSIBLE! Find the opportunity in every place of opposition. If you can't see it, then you will never seize it.

Go back to the drawing board, take out your vision board, and revisit that dream. Make adjustments, review and refine the goal, by developing an action plan to achieve it. If you're waiting until everything is right, until you do something, you'll never do anything. Right now is the right time to launch out with the vision, because provision is waiting for you.

Take care of what is in your control and don't worry about things beyond your control. Work the vision and the provision will come as a result. Fear can never occupy a mindset, that's filled with faith.

You will drive yourself crazy, trying to figure out how God is going to work it out. In the face of adversity, inhale inspiration and exhale empowerment. Breathe and just believe.

DATE OR WAIT?

I like to say, "It may not be your time to date, it just may be your time to wait." While you are waiting, you can't be like a person at a bus stop. You have to be like a person at a restaurant. If you're waiting at a bus stop, you're idle.

At a restaurant, you have positioned yourself as a waitress, because you're serving, preparing, and working for what you anticipate on receiving. While you're waiting, keep working. The word *Wait* does not mean sit and do nothing. Buy yourself some roses. Take yourself to the movies. Go to the gym. Feed your mind with inspiring books. Stay active, rather than remaining idle and isolated. If you stay ready, you won't have to hurry to get ready.

Too many people are afraid to be alone. In fact, alone doesn't mean lonely. Learn to enjoy your own company. When was the last time, you took yourself on a date? When was the last time you bought yourself some flowers, treated yourself to dinner, or the art gallery? Stop allowing your life to collect dust, by waiting for a phone call, text, or an invite from somebody else. RSVP to yourself. If you don't enjoy your own company, why would anybody else?

Oftentimes, people approach relationships looking

to receive rather than to give. You have to approach a

relationship, as a waiter/waitress, rather than as a customer.

When you have the right heart, you look to serve rather than

be served. What can you contribute to others, with a hand

to give rather than to receive? Acts 20:35 affirms, "It is

more blessed to give than to receive. Simply because when

you give, you have already received. It may not always be

expedient or tangible, but your blessing will come.

CHASE YOUR PLAN, NOT A MAN

Don't let society dictate to you, about when you should be

married, how many children you should have, or what you

should aspire to be. Don't let social media fool you.

Everybody who is dating or married, is not happy. A

relationship is not a cure all for loneliness. It's far better to be

alone, than to be with someone who makes you feel alone. If

you have somebody and they're not on your level, then

you're still alone. If we can't relate, then we shouldn't date.

Take the time to date yourself first. Discover your gifts, wants, and needs before seeking data on somebody else. How can someone get to know you, if you don't know you? It's unfair to them and yourself in the long run.

Too many times we ignore the signs, because we are blinded by muscles, money, or a Mercedes. Is he focused on your mind or your behind? What are his intentions? Queen realize that you never have to chase a man, if you have a plan. When you walk in purpose and work your plan, the right man will pursue you. Queen, your feet will always be tired, if you're chasing a man. You were created to strut in heels, not run after a man in gym shoes.

You never have to chase, what you have been chosen to receive. Keep working, loving, giving, and you will begin receiving, the blessing that's intended for you. If you become a person who attracts it, then you won't have to chase it. God is preparing you for it and He's preparing it for you. Just wait on it. Never chase a blessing. If you become a blessing, then blessings will chase you. Focus on God's plan, not a man and the right man will focus on you.

WHAT ARE YOU ATTRACTING?

Do not ignore the fact, that your life is a magnet. Essentially, you will attract the type of person that you are. You are a magnet for the positive or the negative. You repel the good or the bad. What are you attracting based on your attitude, conversation, and mindset?

We don't attract what we want, we attract what we are. If you are negative, mean, angry, and bitter that is what you will attract and as a result, you will be treated as such. You will keep attracting the same type of person, if you're the same old person. On the flip side, when you operate through self-love, a positive mindset, and actions that express those qualities, your life will begin to attract people who exude those attributes.

Until you begin to love yourself, heal old wounds, appreciate your value, and endure growing pains, you will continue to attract the same OLD people in different places, with NEW faces.

You will attract the same type of person, if you're the same type of person. Nothing will change, if you remain the same. The quality of people that you're attracting will change, when you change. In essence, you will attract who and what you are in life. The truth is a hard pill to swallow and many will not digest it easily. Realize that your life is a magnet. When you become a person of love, you will repel the wrong ones and attract the right one.

TAKE ME OUT TO THE BALL GAME

A few months ago, I posted a comedic statement on social

media that wound up going viral. The statement was in response to the Chicago Cubs, who broke their 108 year "curse" by defeating the Cleveland Indians. As a result, the Cubs won the World Series Championship. So, I took to social media and posted, "If the Cubs can wait 108 years to get a ring...ladies you can too! LOL."

I know I'm in trouble with you now. Aren't statements supposed to be funnier, after you put "LOL" after it though? Okay, you're still not laughing. Hear me out though. The feedback and comments felt like a sporting event, because the reactions were mixed with cheers and boos. Some replied, "This is hilarious lol. That's not right LOL." Others expressed, "The devil is a lie. This man got us messed up. I almost cussed him out." Now don't do what they almost did, by cussing me out. Hold your peace.

I realize that baseball and relationships cannot coexist, because too many people play games. Beyond the comedy, comments, and hyperbole to exaggerate "108." The point I was making, is can you wait? Simply because we generally ruin, what we rush. Why do quickly, what you intend to last forever? Don't rush, what God is taking time to prepare.

Society is all about quick fixes and sensationalism. People want fast food, fast WI-FI, speedy success, quick money, fast cars, and then get upset when relationships evolve slowly. Don't be in such a hurry, to get something that may not be worth your time. It's like praying, "Lord give me patience now." Maybe I missed something. If you believe patience is a virtue, then why make rushing the issue? It is far better to wait long, than to marry wrong. Please don't go into a relationship when you're weak, because when you get strong you will say, "What in the world, did I get myself into?"

The flip side of the coin is to never settle, for being an option, when you are a priority. You can never get to the next level, when you settle. In the end, you get less than you deserve. Allow space in a relationship for expression of one's intention. Confusion will always be a crime, when people waste your time. If a man wants you, he will let you know and make provisions to solidify his stance with you. A man that wants you, will never give someone else the opportunity to get you. If he wants you, his actions will reflect in word and deed.

GET THEE BESIDE ME

I attend many soirées and formal dinners, where couples are honored together. Too often, I hear the phrase, "Behind every great man is a great woman." I know it sounds good, but the phraseology of those words is absolutely incorrect. It's not behind, but beside every great man is a great woman. In Genesis 2:21, God put Adam to sleep. As a result, He surgically operated on the man and created Eve, from his rib. I find it interesting that God didn't create the woman from the skull, so she could usurp his authority. God did not create the woman from the plantar bone of the foot, so the man could step on her. Neither did he create the woman from the vertebra of the man's back, so he could be in front of her. Rather God created her from his rib, which is from the side of his anatomical structure. This is because she is intended to be a helpmeet and remain by his side, through times of struggle and strength.

My *Dear Queen,* your King does not have to be in front of you, to lead you. He can do it hand in hand, right by your side. Like a rib protects the heart, a wife protects her husband, just as the husband protects his wife. I believe that a man knows he has found his rib, when he can breathe a lot easier. If you're suffocating or suffering from emphysema, then that may not be the right rib. Don't rush the process, because you will always ruin what your rush. Again, in essence, it's better to wait long than to marry wrong. I'm still waiting to exhale, so pray for me.

If you find yourself *Waiting to Exhale*, here are 3 things to remember:

1. Delay is not Denial.

Waiting for what you want, is better than settling for what you don't want. When you have a vision to go to the next level, you can't afford to settle! Don't wait on someone to create opportunities for you, begin to craft and create your own. Don't give up because what you're expecting, has not happened instantaneously. Some things will not happen until it's time, remember that delay is NOT denial!

2. Work while you're Waiting.

Waiting doesn't mean to just sit back and relax. Waiting comes with expectation, but expectation is forged in the place of experience. It's better to fail going forward, than give up and remain backward. Every failure and disappointment leads you to success. Good things come to those who work, while they wait. Keep working while you're waiting and you will get what you're expecting.

3. **Breathe and Believe.**

Remember that a problem is a solution, waiting to happen. It's up to you to find the answer. The answer is forged in faith not fear. While you're waiting to exhale don't choke, but discover hope. Don't wait for people to do for you, what you can do for yourself. Breathe, believe, and breakthrough!

CHAPTER 4

What's Love Got to Do with It?

You can't express, what you don't possess.
When love fills your heart, there is no space for hate.

T he question goes beyond a catchy, billboard chart

topping, Tina Turner tune. What does love mean to you? I'm

talking about real love. Is it superficial? Is it about what you

can take or what you can give? I'm sure we can agree, that

we need more love in our world. However, it will never be

seen in the world, if it isn't exemplified in our hearts. In fact

it begins with us.

Love isn't a holiday, that starts and stops on

Valentine's Day or Sweetest Day. It should grow stronger

day by day. Gifts don't replace love, for love is the greatest gift. Understand the principle, that you can give without loving, but you can't love without giving. When you show love everyday, then a holiday is just like any other day. Love positions you for the future and propels you, past your past. Roses wilt and chocolates get stale, but only real love lasts.

Some relationships are filled with expensive gifts, but empty hearts. The bracelet became a handcuff, because you're shackled to someone who is not good for you. An empty pocket that has a heart filled with love, is more wealthy than a full pocket, with a heart void of love.

Looking for love in all the wrong places, is not worth it, just to say you have somebody. You don't have to go searching for love. If you become a person of love and reflect the spirit of love, then love will find you. You will attract what you become.

YOU ARE A GIFT

Oftentimes, we get so caught up in giving gifts, that we fail to realize that we are a gift to somebody. Even if it's to ourselves. Indeed love is the only gift, that you can keep giving and never run out of it. You are a red box and a gold bow, a gift to the world. Tangible gifts don't replace love, because love is the greatest gift. You may be alone, but it doesn't mean you have to be lonely. Enjoy your own company. You can never expect anybody to love you, until you start loving yourself.

Even in a world filled with hate, love is still preeminent. Dr. Martin Luther King, Jr. declared, "Hate cannot drive out hate, only love can do that." You can't show love with bitterness, anger, strife, and hatred in your heart. Love and hate cannot occupy the same space, one will cancel out the other.

When you connect to God, He provides you with love under new management. No more games, gimmicks, tricks, or schemes. It's His love for you, out of the depth of who He is, that empowers you to love yourself, love others, and walk in your unique purpose. His love for you reconciles you to Him, yourself, and to those around you.

FRAGILE, DO NOT DROP

Love fills the void in our lives. It begins with embracing God's love and personifying self-love, whereby we can express love to others. This kind of love empowers us to press past hurts, disappointments, abuse, neglect, skeletons in our closets, and the frightening things we fight to overcome. Each one of us, has a "Fragile, do not drop" label on our lives. You never know what people are struggling with internally. Your words and actions don't have a receipt, so you can't take them back. Just be kind, courteous, and handle people with care.

We have all been dropped in various ways, whether by an absentee father, disappointment, or life's situations. From the toughest of us, to the most sensitive, there are places in our lives that need healing, in order to live our best life. You may have been dropped and damaged, but God can repair and fix your heart.

BOOMERANG

Love has a boomerang effect; the more love you share with others, the more it comes back to you. Love is more than just a word and it intensifies when we give it mean. Love is not about what it says, love is about what it does. Love doesn't neglect, it protects. Love is not selfish, it's selfless.

Remember that real love, is about more than finding a perfect person. Real love is about learning to love an imperfect person, perfectly. Real love can drive out hate. Real love can transform death into life. Real love can transform stumbling blocks into stepping stones. Real love can help a hurting hater. Real love can be good to somebody who was never good to you. When God's love is the

blueprint, it provides a boomerang effect as imperfect people

become perfect for one another.

LISTENING IS NOT WAITING TO TALK

In the matrix of relationships, communication must be a

foundational element to sustain it. There is no way that you

can spell *Communication*, without *U* and *I*. It takes a

committed tandem and teamwork to communicate. The

building block of communication, is the foundational

framework, for the development of that relationship. Whether

in business, dating, or marriage, good communication is

necessary.

A lack of communication can suffocate a relationship,

but good communication can breathe life into it. One of the

biggest communication mistakes we make, is when we listen

to reply, instead of listening to understand. Listening is not, waiting to talk!

As men and women communicate, we need to understand that the essence of communication is not solely about your ability to speak. It's more importantly about your ability to listen. It's not so much about what you say, it's about listening to what is being said. Communication and comprehension, are essential components to relational compatibility. A relationship should present an olive branch for peace, not a grudge match to fight. Practice communicating and listening, instead of arguing.

SILENCE IS GOLDEN

For any relationship to have success, you have to talk, but you also have to listen. Both are intertwined in the art of communication. I believe that women, are the stronger communicative beings. Women communicate from a feeling perspective and men from a fact based approach. Neither is more correct than the other, however men and women are just wired differently. As men we have been taught to repress our feelings. Women on the other hand, are given space to express their feelings. As a result women are generally, stronger in the art of communicating how they feel. We don't always receive it, but it doesn't negate the fact, that ladies are good at it. I tell brothers all the time, "You will never win, by arguing with a woman."

The ability to communicate can be an asset, as opposed to a liability when used carefully. Do you have the composure to listen and hear, beyond what your eyes can only see? Don't just listen to what people are saying, listen to what they are not saying. It takes discipline to listen and be silent. It's interesting that the words, "Listen and silent" have the same letters, yet both are priceless words. Our words are like swords that can chop somebody, or sharpen them. We must use them wisely, as we communicate daily. Sometimes it's best not to say anything, if you're going to say the wrong thing. Silence is golden, learn how to be precious.

MOTIVE FOR MARRIAGE

For the record, *wifey* and wife are two separate meanings. Yet, cohabitation is on the rise and since 1960, there are eight times as many out of wedlock births.

How do you introduce the relevance of marriage, to an "I'm doing me generation?" Is it still possible to say, "I do" in an iPad, iPhone, iPod, and YouTube generation? We're living in a world today, that spells the word "We" with two "I's." I'm referring to the "Wii" video game system.

Even the names of our techno gadgets, are indicative of a narcissistic ideology. In an age that says, "It's all about I and you" can the focus still be on "Us and we?" How can you build a long-lasting marriage, in an instant gratification society? We see that people aren't waiting seven years, to scratch their itch any longer.

If you desire to be married, what is your motive? Is it love, money, loneliness, sense of obligation, sex, control, age, or other factors? Some people marry only for the wedding or a social media photo op. Marriage is not a quick fix. It's not a sprint, it's a marathon. It's not a race, it's a pace. Marriage is a merger. Marriage is not a taste test or product, with a money back guarantee. It's a life-long investment. If you don't have the right partner, or make the right investments, your marriage will eventually go bankrupt.

A number of women flaunt their body, while many men parade their money. After the rendezvous is over she cries, "He only wanted me for my body" and he says, "She only wanted my money." Well, if that's all you showcased and promoted, then that's all you will attract. Bring more to the table than an appetite.

If you don't remedy the damaging relationships of the

past, it will bring about a jaded perspective for the future.

Now when it's time for marriage, the man shouts like Kanye

West, "We want prenup, we want prenup." Read me clearly,

"I'm not saying she's a gold digger, but she ain't messing with

no"...I think you get my point.

Queens are goal diggers, not gold diggers because they

value themselves. What are your values? If you're

exchanging your self-worth and character in hopes of karats,

you will face the spectrum of disappointment. If you have to

give an ultimatum, bribe to be a bride, or beg a man to marry

you, then you will have to do all of that and more to keep

him from straying or leaving you. I'm beginning to realize,

that marriage is not solely about finding someone that you

can live with, it's about loving someone that you can't live

without.

LOVE IN 4D

In scripture, the 13th chapter of I Corinthians expresses, "Love is patient, love is kind. Love does not envy or keep a record of wrongs." The passage affirms, that you can be intoxicated with the exuberance of your intellectual verbosity, to where you speak with royal eloquence and angelic ecstasy. However, none of it matters if you're negative, hateful, and bitter. When you express that you love something or someone, what does that mean? How do you define love?

In relationships, it's worth asking, "Do I love you the way I love or do I love you, the way that you need to be loved?" So many are in search of what real love entails. There are a plethora of expressions and interpretations for love. The English interpretation to define love, is very limited and narrow in its approach. For instance you can say, "I love your dress, I love my dog, I love my husband" and there be no exact definition to distinguish the meaning, because it's limited within the scope of its interpretation.

The Greeks analyzed love in four dimensions, from a panoramic perspective using the words: Eros, Philia, Storge, and Agape. Each word has its own unique meaning, being applicable to our lives.

Eros is passionate love, with sensual desire and longing. The modern Greek word, "Erotas" means intimate love, where we derive the word "Erotic" for sensual passion.

Philia means friendship or affectionate love. It includes loyalty to family, friends, and community. It's also rooted, in the etymological name of the city of Philadelphia, which means "Brotherly love."

Storge is natural affection, expressed by parents for their children. The Greeks used Storge to describe relationships within the family.

God doesn't operate in Eros, Philia, or Storge, He

operates in Agape. The terms Eros, Phila, and Storge describe love with limits. However, **Agape** has no limitations because it's rooted in unconditional love. Agape is love without limits and the deepest form of love.

LIMITLESS LOVE

As a human being with limitations and frailties, can you love someone unconditionally? Think about that for a minute. Do you have the capacity, to love without limits and conditions? I would suggest, emphatically no.

The Bible never commands us to love unconditionally, because God knows that we are finite and flawed. However, He commands us to exemplify and express love to each other, even through our flawed mechanics.

Every relationship has a deal breaker. Don't act like yours doesn't. Even if it's not communicated and expressed, it is thought about. You have said to yourself, "If he ever does this, I'm out." Some things you can tolerate, but other things are intolerable. The only one, who can love without limits and express love unconditionally, is God.

You and I, are too flawed to love unconditionally. You can have the intent to love, but it must entail the extent, that goes beyond finite limitations. The more connected we are to God, the more His love is able to flow through us. As a result, we can look beyond the conditions and shortcomings of others, to embrace their needs. Why are we so quick to impute judgment and punish others, for what we seek forgiveness and mercy for ourselves? You may have never killed anyone, but you thought about it. You didn't steal the purse or earrings, but you played out the scenario in your mind. If God looked beyond your faults and saw your needs, then surely you can do the same for someone else.

LOVE UNDER NEW MANAGEMENT

Let's be an example of love, according to the love letter in

I Corinthians 13, which declares, "Love is patient, love is kind, love is never jealous, and love is not envious." When we understand the power of love and God's love, then we can love ourselves and express love to each other. When you live in love under new management, it frees you from your past. Love empowers you to forgive those who hurt you and gives you peace to move forward, knowing that the best is yet to come. Love liberates. Its power will forgive those who would never give you an apology, because forgiveness is freedom.

So, what's love got to do with it? Everything! You can't express, what you don't possess. When love fills your heart, there is no space for hate. Love is strong enough to find peace, from broken pieces. Romans 8:38 persuades us to know that love is too strong for death to outlast it, too extensive for life to outlive it, too majestic for angels, principalities, and powers to dominate it. Love is too far beyond, for the present or future to blockade it. Love is too high and wide, for you to get around it.

LESSONS IN LOVE

Love is more than just a word and it intensifies, when we give it meaning. Love is not about what it says, love is about what it does. See love through a different lens. Take time to meditate and recognize the attributes of love:

Love never gives up.

Love cares more for others than self.

Love doesn't want what it doesn't have.

Love doesn't strut.

Love isn't puffed up.

Love is selfless, not selfish.

Love doesn't keep a record of wrongs.

Love doesn't revel in seeking revenge.

Love takes pleasure in truth.

Love always looks for the best, not the worst.

Love never looks back, it always looks forward.

Love lifted you and me.

Love keeps going to the end.

Love will always win.

CHAPTER 5

Heal Before You Deal

You can't truly heal from it, until you deal with it.

Have you ever been emotionally, psychologically, relationally, or spiritually broken? Just limping through life. Smiling on the outside, hurting on the inside to where you cry yourself to sleep, night after night.

FROM PROCESS, TO PROGRESS

As a survivor of stage 4 cancer, I'm a living witness that healing is not always an event, sometimes it's a process. The process of being healed takes time, patience, and commitment. You can be dealing with scars and wounds, while healing from them at the same time. As God is healing you, He is revealing greater strength in you.

One of the greatest consolations, is in knowing, there is a purpose through the process. There is a message through the mess and a testimony through your test. The strength discovered in life, derives from how you handle what you go through. I'm a believer that 10 percent of life is what happens to us, 90 percent is how we proactively move forward, as a result. There are things that you may never get over, they just have to be managed. More than just going through, you have to GROW through every hurt and disappointment.

HURTING PEOPLE, HURT PEOPLE

You may say, "I've been hurt and I don't know, if I can ever love again." Yes we have been hurt, but we have also hurt others too. I'm sure you have heard the expression, "Hurting people, hurt people." There is much truth and pain, in the simplicity of the statement. Simply because, if the hurt within has not been healed, it will flow through one's life and afflict others. Some people have become so numb to pain, that it hurts to be happy. On the contrary, healed people, heal people and loving people, love other people. What flows through you, is a direct reflection of what is in you. When you take the time to deal with the hurt, you can heal from it.

SOUL FOOD

When you heal from the hurt, abuse, neglect, and lack of love from the inside, you will stop attracting the type of people who bring those issues on the outside. Your life is a magnet and you will attract the type of people that you are. The negative people that you attract, are riddled with the issues, that you're dealing with from within. Taking time to let God heal you, is food for your mind and soul. It serves as a remedy to the malady that you're facing. Healing puts your life in proximity with your purpose, adding harmony to your destiny.

FROM GREAT MESS, TO GREATNESS

Only God can transform a great mess into greatness. Use your pain as poetry and allow your malady, to become your greatest melody. You can survive and thrive in spite of heartbreak, loss, and broken relationships. Realize that what God has brought you through, is an indication of where He can take you. Let the past go, so you can grow. Forgive, so you can live your best life. Your great mess will become a great message of transformation.

NO MORE DRAMA

Rid yourself of toxic relationships, drama, and negativity. This is your time to take inventory. Evaluate and terminate those who are relational roadblocks. You need connectors and collaborators who will lift you up, not bring you down. Remember, if they're talking behind your back, that means you are ahead of them. If they're trying to bring you down, it's because they are below you. Don't stoop to their level. People may have hurt you, but don't let it break your spirit. You're stronger than the forces against you. As former First Lady of the United States, Michelle Obama declared, "When they go low, we go high." Keep rising higher, to soar to the next level.

THE MANNEQUIN CHALLENGE

If you haven't heard of it, *The Mannequin Challenge* is a viral social media video trend, where people remain frozen in action like mannequins as a video is recorded. From politicians to pro athletes, millions of people have struck a pose when the music plays or at the count of three. It can be fun to act like a mannequin, but it's frightening to be lifeless like a mannequin. Too many people will take *The Mannequin Challenge* but not step up to the challenge in their calling, community, and career for success.

The sad reality is that much like a mannequin, people go through life faking it. Frozen in their past, refusing to make any moves. You can't go through life faking it and being a mannequin, you've got to keep it real. You can't keep it real with anybody else, until you first keep it real with yourself. To do that takes accountability, honesty, and a willingness to admit your mistakes. Will you take on the challenge of loving your enemies? Will you step up to the challenge, of working your gifts and purpose? Will you embrace the challenge, of loving yourself and seeing the greatness in you, despite what has happened to you? Stop holding the mannequin pose, it's time to get moving.

THE "S" ON YOUR CHEST

Dear Queen, I'm sure that you can confess, the "S" on your chest, doesn't always symbolize Superwoman, success, or strength. Sometimes the "S" on your chest, means sensitivity, sadness, or struggle. Many times the struggle is with insecurity, identity, feeling incomplete, addiction, or abandonment. Society has taught us to repress our feelings, rather than express them. So, for years we harbor feelings of anger, resentment, unhappiness, and bitterness all while searching for purpose, and the reality of what it means to be a Queen.

COVER GIRL

Oftentimes we look for things to cover our pain and mask our brokenness, without going to the deeper heart of the issue. All of the makeup in the world, can't cover a saddened soul. Mascara and Maybelline can't cover the hurt and shame, that makes you writhe in pain. Drowning your sorrows in a bottle, will only drown your heart in deeper misery. Trying to smoke it away, will only serve as a smoke screen to hide what's inside. Going to the club, will only make you feel alone, to where you find yourself dancing with the devil. You can't hear the voice within you, until you mute the noise around you. We all have issues. You can't continue to put a bandaid, over what is hemorrhaging in your life. God has the remedy for our malady. When you cast your cares on Him and give Him your issues, then He will uncover what you have tried to cover. He will give you healing tissues for your hurting issues, to help you recover.

PRETTY HURTS

In her song, *Pretty Hurts*, Beyoncé underscores the pain of a girl/woman who tries to fit the mold that society sets. From her hair to her hips, the lack of love and continued insecurity produces pain. The melody casts a light on a life, that lacks harmony and unity, with itself. Mrs. Knowles-Carter, mellifluously, melodiously and euphoniously, echoes the lyrics, "Pretty hurts, we shine the light on whatever's worst. Trying to fix something, but you can't fix what you can't see. It's the soul that needs the surgery."

You can't fix on the outside that which needs a makeover on the inside. Healing has to happen within or you will forever be without love for self. Oftentimes, life makes us so numb to pain, that it hurts to be happy. Remove yourself from the hands that broke you, to make room for the hands that will bless you. Take the light off your flaws and shine it on your strengths. You don't fit the mold. God broke the mold when He created you. Love your flaws and the skin you're in. Somebody is waiting to love the flaws that you hate, but you have to love yourself first. Yes, pretty hurts but beauty is coming out of your pain.

DELIVERED BUT NOT HEALED

You can be delivered, but not healed. What I mean is that, you're no longer in the situation that brought pain, but your mind and heart are still battling with the pain. You can be out of a situation, but your mind is still trapped and connected to the hurt. Physically you are free, but you're psychologically incarcerated because there is brokenness within. Healing is not an overnight instance, it's a continual process. When you begin to trust God and experience His love, there will be healing that flows through your life. God will show you how to love yourself and as a result, love others.

GOOD IN GOODBYE

Don't let the pain from an EX, prevent you from receiving the love from your NEXT. It didn't work out right, because they were the wrong one. Your ex, became the example of how to let go to grow. To be in a position to receive the right one, you have to disconnect from the wrong one. Stop projecting the issues from past relationships, onto people who had nothing to do with it. Sometimes your experience with the wrong person, sets you up for the right one. The right one will see, what the wrong one was blind to. When it's the right one, love won't be the question, it will be the answer.

Let the hurt, pain, and baggage go. Relationships are like boarding an airplane, too much baggage is going to cost you. Refuse to be bitter, because better is coming. Bless and release, what was never meant to last. You can't marry your future, until you divorce your past. When you're healed, you won't wish them hell. You will wish them well. When you find the good in goodbye, you can look back and laugh at the past. In you they lost the best, but it was only a setup to experience the blessed.

When you look back, thank your past for the lessons.

Your future brought you greater blessings. Leave the past in the past. Some people were only apart of your history, but not apart of your destiny. Stop recycling, what God is replacing. Start preparing for the one, that God is preparing for you. This time it won't be a mismatch, but your hearts will make the perfect match. Release your past, so you can embrace your future. When there's a divine love connection, no one can separate the state of your perfect union. Have the courage to say goodbye to the past, so you can say hello to your future.

ATTRACT AND REPEL

The right relationships will add to you and multiply your value. Start attracting the positive and repelling the negative. Love yourself! You have greatness, peace, and joy within. You're pregnant with purpose, promise, possibility, and potential. Give birth to it and walk in healing. No amount of money or material possessions, can determine your value. You, yes YOU are priceless. Know your worth. Appreciate who you are. Embrace your gifts. Live with purpose, on purpose, and for a purpose. Love yourself and reveal your greatness within. You will begin to live your dream, when you rid yourself of the drama that weighs you down.

In many cases, to deal with someone new, you have to heal the old wounds. You can't repel what you're attracting, if you're still the same person that's attracting the same people.

PAINFUL BUT PURPOSEFUL

Some time ago, my mother had an inadvertent accident and injured her foot. During her visit to the podiatrist, she received an X-ray. The doctor evaluated the results and told her, "I have some good and bad news. The bad news is that your ankle is broken, but the good news is that it's in the perfect position to heal." You need to realize that despite

what has happened to you or what you have experienced, you

are still in the perfect position to heal.

The opposition you're facing, is positioning you in the

perfect place to pray. Sometimes the devil has you, right

where God wants you to be. What the enemy used to break

you, God will use the pain to heal you. Yes it was painful, but

it became purposeful in order for you to be successful.

WOUNDS TO WISDOM

The same old wounds will open in a new relationship, if

you don't heal from the old ones. You have to heal the old,

before you deal with the new. When you heal it reveals

greater vision within, to look at love through a different lens.

When love begins from within, your parameters widen and

you become a magnet for love. You will continue to wreck

people's lives and yours in the process, until you take the

time to heal. When God heals you, don't pick at the wound.

Take time and allow yourself to heal, before you deal with

someone new.

CHAPTER 6

Red Box, Gold Bow

The tragedy is to be gifted, but never open the package.

Never fail to recognize that YOU are a gift. Your treasure within; your talents, testimony, tenacity, trials, and triumphs are unique to who you are, as a champion within. Realize that you are a red box and a gold bow, a true gift to the world.

The famous painter, Pablo Picasso declared, "The meaning of life is to find your gift, the purpose of life is to give your gift away." The tragedy in life, is to be gifted but never open the package. So many people are gifted, yet never open their package to reveal their true treasure. Being blessed with gifts, but never using them, therein lies the tragedy.

GIFTED FOR GREATNESS

God created you as His gift to the world. God's gift to you is wrapped in the package of life. What you do with your life is a gift to God. You were born to manage, maintain, and manifest your destiny. Your life is not void of what you need to succeed. You are pre-packaged with intelligence, energy, passion, tenacity, creativity, ingenuity, and resilience to thrive everyday that you're alive. Begin to recognize your greatness. The greatest part of you, can't be seen with the eyes, it must be discerned by the heart. Dig deep, within the soil of your soul and bless the world with your inner value. You are gifted for greatness.

THE GREATEST GIFT

Love is the only gift, that you can keep giving and never run out of it. Love is the ultimate gift that keeps on giving. God's love is a gift to you. Each day, you are able to unwrap it and use it to bless others with it. How do you use the gift of love to bring change to your community? We are in need of it. You are the leader that you have been looking for, with the answers to the questions that so many people ask.

STIR IT UP

Never despise the day of small beginnings. Successful people do not start on the mountaintop, they toil in the valley. Oftentimes, they are told "No" countless times. However, they refuse to give up, because "No" means "New opportunity." They view rejection as redirection, to push them in the right direction toward the goal.

This is the same mindset that you have to adopt, in order to stir up your God-given gifts. No one will do it for you, but you have to change your mindset and press past your comfort zone. How much longer will you wait and procrastinate? You have too many gifts in you, to let it all go to waste. Time doesn't wait for the perfect you. So, why are you waiting for the perfect time? Now is the time!

TALKERS VS. WORKERS

There is always a fine line, between talkers and workers. People will talk about you, whether you succeed or fail. Keep working while they are talking and let your success make noise. Don't go seeking revenge, your success will be the greatest revenge, because you put in the hard work when everyone else partied, wasted time, kept their face glued to the phone, and talked behind your back. Men lie, women lie, but results don't lie.

BIG APPLE, BIG DELAY

Recently I was in New York, to speak at an event for professionals in business, politics, and education. It seemed as if I was never going to get to the Big Apple, because my journey to New York City, was met with delay after delay. It was absolutely frustrating. How do you respond when frustration, seems to overtake your focus? When it appears that you're regressing, more than you're progressing?

Have you ever felt that everybody seems to be getting ahead, while you're left behind? It seems as if everybody is getting married, but you're still single. Everyone around you is getting a promotion, but you're still in the same position. Every other entrepreneur has gone global, but you're still struggling local. Don't worry, don't fret, don't get fickle in your faith, but remain focused! Trust and believe that the harvest of opportunity awaits those, who refuse to be weary and lose heart.

It seemed as if, I was never going to get to New York, in the appropriate time frame. My flight was cancelled and rescheduled. The plane didn't take off at its designated time, and my patience seemed to be turning into frustration. If you've never felt dismayed, discombobulated, and disappointed, then I'm not talking to you.

As I sat on the plane, we just continued to go in circles on the runway, without taking flight through the air. Have you ever been in a place, where life had you going in circles, but you weren't making progress? You were seeking to soar, but something was clipping your wings.

THOUGHTS BECOME THINGS

It becomes imperative to not think negative, when things are negative or it will remain negative. You must transform your mind to think positive in a negative situation, in order to transform your circumstance. What God has for you, is uniquely designed just for you. If you lean to your own understand, you will fall. Trust Him, so you can stand through trying times. Tough times don't last, only tough people do.

TIMING IS EVERYTHING

Realize that some things will not happen, until it's the right time. Delay does not mean denial. Keep believing while you're waiting. While you're waiting, it's no time for crying and quitting. It's your time to keep working. Don't make a temporary decision, out of weakness. It will cost you more going nowhere, then it will to go somewhere. Waiting on God is never a waste of time. When it's His will, it will happen at the right time.

REVELATION IN YOUR SITUATION

Look beyond your situation, for revelation. See the positive in the negative. Things will remain the same, only if you think the same. You will soar into the right opportunity at the right time. When things aren't working for you, then it's time for you to work on you. When you do, the right things will happen at the right time. Remain introspective and take personal inventory, as you anticipate the right opportunity.

Remember that God is always on time, even when we think

He's late.

GIFTED BUT AFFLICTED

If you're gifted, you will be afflicted. The adversity that you

endure is a setup for your next level. The greater the battle,

the greater your blessing. If you're facing much adversity,

know that much more opportunity is ahead for you. Great

breakthroughs, are always a result of great burdens. Don't let

a setback set you back, have the faith to bounce back. There

is a gift in you, that the world is waiting for you to reveal. If

you can endure the test, your testimony will be great. If you

can hold fast and endure the affliction, your elevation will be

greater.

JEWEL OR JUNK?

According to the retail store *Forever 21*, the average woman consumes six pounds of lipstick in her lifetime. Yes, your lipstick and lip gloss is popping, but is your language stopping you from progressing?

Dear Queen, more important than what covers your lips, is what flows from your lips. Proverbs 20:15 affirms, "The lips of knowledge are a precious jewel." Beautiful lips that utter ugly words, make you look unattractive.

What does the content of your conversation consist of? Are you spending time hating or elevating others? Are you gossiping or getting things done? When you're a jewel, you don't allow junk you to flow from your lips.

Far too often, we have to unravel the junk in our lives to find the jewel within. Don't look around, for what you already possess within. It's already in you. Dig deeper through the hurt, pain, struggle, abuse, neglect, depression, and you will find the resources that you need. Place your value in God's hands, not in the hands of those who fail to realize it. If they treat other people like trash, what makes you think they will treat you like a jewel? The jewel in you, doesn't have space to occupy junk. Rid yourself of it and rise above it.

CHAPTER 7

Break The Cycle

Stop breathing life into dead relationships.
Don't resuscitate and give CPR,
to things that should receive a eulogy.

Are you continually in toxic relationships, getting your heartbroken, and being left depleted? It's not always somebody else's fault. A lot of times we are at fault, because of what we allow people to do to us. People will treat you, by the way you allow them to treat you. When you take inventory of your life, you are able to set standards, goals, principles, and values for living. You give people a blueprint, of how to treat you, by the way you treat yourself. You have to teach people, how to treat you and not allow them to mistreat you.

ENTER OR EXIT

Stop allowing people to treat you like an entrance and exit, walking in and out of your life. Sometimes you have to shut the door, to find out if they're temporary or permanent. Don't live your life doing permanent things, with temporary people. It places you in a state of bitterness, discontent, and brokenness because you will spend your life, trying to recover from the hurt that you have experienced. The right person will do more than tell you that they love you, they will show you. Simply because, there is a fine line between real love and lip service. Lip service leaves you with broken promises. Real love is exemplified through consistency in one's actions.

There's an old school song that says, "You've got me going in circles, round and round I go." You can never make forward progress, if you're continually going in circles day after day. Break the cycle of brokenness, toxic relationships, abuse, drama, depression, negativity, bitterness, and strife.

STEP IN THE NAME OF LOVE

If you stay in step with God, the right person will step in your life, for a lifetime. They won't come to take, but give. They don't intend to hurt, only to help you, because they want the best for you.

The season of doing permanent things, with temporary people is over. Let it go. Seek God's heart, not His hand and the right man with a plan, will seek God's heart for your hand.

God has a rhythm. When you stay in beat with his timing, the right connection will happen at the right time. *Dear Queen*, what God has prepared for you, is far greater than what has happened to you. Stay in step with His purpose and plan for your life. As you pursue your purpose, the right man will pursue you. Before you put your heart in a man's hands, make sure his heart is securely in God's hands. He will love, lead, and lift you to the next level. Dance with God and He will let the right man cut in, to dance with you forever, on your journey to destiny. As you stay in step with God, He will release the love that lasts for a lifetime.

MAJOR KEY

There is a door of opportunity that God wants you to step into. However, it comes at the expense and even the pain of breaking away from your past. Closing the door on your past, gives you the keys to open the door to your limitless future.

Shut the door on relationships that have kept you discombobulated, depressed, and defeated. It's simple to say, but it takes courage to do it. Break the cycle of bad habits, toxic relationships, stinking thinking, and low level living. Your gifts are the keys, to break out of the old and unlock the new doors of destiny.

TOXIC RELATIONSHIPS

They say, "It's not what you walk away from, it's what you walk away with." Many of us have walked away from toxic relationships, but we have walked away with a broken heart, emotional baggage, scars of abuse, mistrust, depression, and low self-esteem. These were not parting gifts, but curses that seek to destroy your life and the generations to come. Give yourself the gift of healing and forgiveness, to break the curse of bitterness and brokenness. Forgive whoever hurt you and forgive yourself, for allowing it to happen.

Realize that toxic relationships, are a biohazard to your breakthrough and purpose. Toxic connections and negative relationships are unhealthy, which will in turn destroy your life. Toxic relationships will not only cause you heartbreak and heartache, but heartburn and heart attack.

You don't need a whole bunch of people in your life, you just need the right people. The right people and relationships won't reduce you, they will produce greater purpose in you. Never reduce yourself, to fit in with people who don't like you anyway. The people who try to reduce you, can see in you what you don't see in yourself. They can see your purpose and potential. As a result, they will try to destroy you, so that you don't walk in your God-given greatness.

When God is for you, the who that are against you don't even matter. When God favors you, people who don't like you, can't do anything about it. Be cognizant of who is in your circle. Major dreamers, don't associate themselves with minor thinkers and dream killers.

R.I.P.

Stop trying to breathe life into dead relationships. Don't resuscitate and give CPR to things, that should receive a eulogy. Oftentimes those dead relationships become dead weight in your life. The only way to grow, is to let it go. I know it sounds easier than it is. There are two ways to look at it. You can either deal with the nagging pain of a bad relationship or you can break it off and breakthrough.

Yes, there will be pain either way. It's your decision, if you decide to stay locked into a relationship of distrust, abuse, sadness, and arguments. You're not on a debate team, why are you arguing all the time? Breaking it off may lead to a moment of breakdown, but eventually you will breakthrough.

WHINING OR WINNING?

You may cry because it's over, but the tears you shed are watering the seeds for your harvest. Don't cry over the man who left. Rejoice about the one, who will celebrate the Queen in you. Refuse to be bitter about how someone treated you. Stop whining and start winning. Get better because the right one will love and embrace you. Be patient through the process. The right one won't hold you back, they will have your back and empower you to move forward. A Queen knows that a King has her back.

MAKE CHANGES FOR CHANGE

They say, "If it ain't broke, don't fix it." How can you improve your life, if you don't take inventory of your life? A lot of times we wait until things are in disarray, to make changes, to the extent that we ignore the signals and red flags along the way.

Take time to analyze your life and relationships. Who or what is a liability versus an asset? Don't wait until things are broken in your life, to remediate and repair certain issues. Do personal inventory with introspection and inspection. If you want to see changes, then you have to make changes.

Break the cycle of lethargy and take time to fix, mend, and repair before it breaks you.

ENOUGH IS ENOUGH

There comes a time, when you have to get sick and tired of being sick and tired, in order to move forward. Does it seem as if you're making no forward progress, you're going in a revolving door of stagnation, and life has become mundane? A good friend and mentor, Mr. Trabian Shorters (CEO of BMe) says, "Change starts, when excuses stop."

Are you making excuses or are you making changes? If you only get hung up on what's negative, you'll remain in a place of negativity. Begin to look at the negative, positively. You literally have to get to a place that says, "Enough Is Enough." I've had enough negativity. I've experienced enough mediocrity, that it's now time for me to maximize my moment and pursue my purpose.

In order to shift the paradigm, you have to be willing to shake up your space. You know it's time to shake up things, when negativity becomes your norm and lack becomes your lifestyle. To break the cycle, takes personal inventory that analyzes your mentality, relationships, spiritual connection, health, daily habits, vision, etc. You can't have a million dollar dream, with a mediocre mindset.

You won't experience any breakthroughs, if you're only looking to be comfortable. At the END of your comfort zone, is the BEGINNING of your breakthrough. What do you need to let go? What do you need to latch ahold to? Your haters are not your worst enemies, it's YOU. If you refuse to get out of your own way, then you are impeding your progress to success and becoming your worst enemy.

You're more than your situation. You're more than a negative experience, or a broken relationship. God has more in store for you. It's time to roll up your sleeves, stir up your gifts, and pursue your purpose with passion. Rid yourself of anybody and anything, that's holding you back. You can't afford to carry around dead weight. Tell yourself, "Enough is Enough." You have had enough negativity and mess. It's time to postion yourself for the positive, through growth and productivity.

SUBSTANCE OR SUPERFICIALITY?

I know you made your list and checked it twice. Maybe you want a man who is six feet, makes six figures, and has a six pack. Beware, all those sixes may leave you with a devil. Recognize and realize, that you can still be with a brother that's 5'10" and win. You're focused on how he looks and what he has, when that all may be superficial. Beyond his looks, does he have leadership? Does he treat you like a Queen? Does he respect you? Does he have a relationship with God? Does he intend to build a future with you?

Like no house can have a firm foundation built on sand, no relationship can thrive without substance. You need more than style, you need something to stand on, when the storms of life come your way.

When you begin to change your mindset, the parameters of your life begin to increase. You begin to see past the superficial, through the real lens of who people are and that is through the lens of love.

WHAT'S THE TEMPERATURE?

Conversations and questions about the temperature or weather, happen daily in your community and are expressed by the meteorologist on TV. If you live in Detroit like me, then you know it's likely to be hot, cold, rainy, snowy, and windy all in a span of a few hours. The deeper concept of temperature that I'm referencing, isn't solely based on degrees, it's primarily about decisions.

Your approach to life must be like a thermostat, rather than a thermometer. A thermometer merely reflects the temperature, but a thermostat sets the temperature. You are not here to reflect the circumstances and situations, that surround your life. Your purpose is to set the atmosphere and change the climate, of the circumstances that you face. Too many people are fickle and fair-weather. They are only happy, when things are going well and the sun is shining at a balmy 82 degrees. Some people only feel good, when their name is being called and when they have red bottom heels on their feet.

Can you still find serenity and solace through the storms of life, when it's cloudy, rainy, and frigid? Can you still remain positive, in negative situations? You can, when you know this too shall pass. Simply because, happiness is based on what's happening around you. However, joy becomes the standard to shift the temperature and set the atmosphere for your life, based on what's inside of you. When you can see beyond what you see, you realize that dark times often lead to brighter opportunities. It's not about what's on you or around you, it's about what's in you that will give you the victory.

You don't need fair-weather friends, you need someone to stick with you through thick and thin. Fickle and fair-weather folk, allow their situation to dictate to them, rather than dictating to their situation. Who is in control? You or your circumstances? Stop telling God, how big your situation is and start telling your situation, how big God is in the midst of it! Now that takes faith. It doesn't have to be gigantic faith, because all you need is mustard seed faith to speak to your situation. Your confession will ultimately determine your possession, or lack thereof.

Don't be reactive, be proactive. You are not a responder, you are an initiator. You are not a thermometer, you're a thermostat. When the temperature is extremely frigid or fiery, just know that victory is on the way. I don't know what the temperature will be tomorrow. I don't know the circumstances that are ahead for tomorrow. I don't know what the future holds. I do know who holds the future and I don't have to worry. Just like a thermostat, the atmosphere is already set for your victory.

BRUISED BUT NOT BROKEN

For as long as I can remember, I have always been encouraged by stories of struggle and strength. The desire to find courage in discouraging times, has always inspired me to reach higher. Much of which is directly connected to the battles, that I have had to face.

One day, I came across an interview with comedian Sheryl Underwood. She is a very opinionated Queen of comedy. I listened to her share about being a candidate, for a prospective tour with notable female comedians. Sheryl shared that she was on a conference call. Right before she pressed the button to speak, she was taken aback by the hurtful comments being made about her on the phone. She couldn't believe that notable comedians, were insulting her based on her size and skin complexion.

Rather than press the button to speak, she decided to hang up the phone instead. Now, I don't know about you, if that had been me in Sheryl's place, I probably would have pressed the button. I know you're above all of that, but I would have said, "Hey, what was that? Come again?" Maybe a few other choice words too. I still have some growing up to do. One day I'll be on your level. In the meantime, pray for a brother. *Dear Queen*, please pray for a King.

Sheryl went on to share that for many years, she would cross paths with those same people who talked about her. Rather than pick a fight and address the individuals, she treated them with kindness. They didn't know Sheryl heard it, but she knew they said it. As Sheryl was on TV sharing her story, she said, "They bruised me, but they didn't break my spirit." What a powerful and profound example of perseverance.

They didn't break Sheryl's spirit, because she didn't allow them to. Much like Sheryl, we have been knocked down by hurtful words, betrayal, abuse, and heartbreak. Don't stay down, get back up! A knockdown is not a knockout, unless you stay down. You may be at your breaking point, but you will breakthrough if you don't breakdown.

It's not just what you go through, it's how you GROW through what you go through. The greater the pain, the greater your purpose. Grow through every place of adversity, because opportunity awaits you on the other side. You have what it takes to overcome. The situation may have bruised you. The circumstance may have crippled you. The people may have betrayed you, but don't let it break you.

God will heal you from every bruise and place of brokenness. I know they hurt you, but heal. I know they treated you with hate, but love again. I know they knocked you down, but get up. Don't allow bitterness to reside within your mind and heart. Let love replace the hate. When love fills your heart, there is no space for hate. It's strong enough to turn broken pieces, into masterpieces. You know what to do. Break the cycle and breakthrough. Move forward with expectation. God is going to give you the last laugh, in the face of your enemies.

CHAPTER 8

Focus On Your Focus

It's better to do one or two things in excellence, than seven or eight things average. Focus on your focus.

Your level of focus has everything to do, with stagnation or progression in life. Don't take detours to destruction, via distractions. Vision gives you clear direction, to avoid detours and distractions altogether. Remain focused! When you're focused, you can still find clarity, when things are cloudy.

IMPOSSIBLE OR I'M POSSIBLE?

This is your time to focus, plan, and execute your vision to perfection. Target the goal and execute the plan. It's better to do one or two things in excellence, than seven or eight things average. Focus on your focus. If you only focus on the obstacle, then you will never see the opportunity. Great opportunities are in store for you, if you work while you wait! It's all about perception. You can either see challenges, as impossible or "I'm possible." Hard work and tenacity, will make your dream a reality.

Place the right people around you, who understand your drive and energy. They won't discourage you from the goal, they will encourage you to achieve the goal. The right people will breathe easy, when you get blessed and not suffocate on your success. Focus on how God has blessed you, not the people that stress you. Focus on Him, not them. Make focus your priority, not people.

FOCUS FORWARD

There is too much ahead, to focus on what you left behind. You're too blessed, to focus on what you don't have. Look at what you do have and use it! Look forward and move forward. Your feet will propel you, in the direction where your eyes are focused. You can't go through life looking and walking backward, or you will crash into your past. If they only knew who you were becoming, they wouldn't focus on what you used to be. Focus forward. What's past is past, your future is promising.

THE BLESSED IS YET TO COME

In order to look forward, stop looking around and behind you. God's got your back, so goodness and mercy are always following you. Raise your faith and your level of focus. Commit to the plan, develop action steps, and work to bring your vision to fruition. If your mind and will is committed to it, you can't lose. Remind yourself that the best and blessed is yet to come.

FINE-TUNE YOUR FOCUS

Stop focusing on what's stressful, look within and use your gifts to be successful. The gift in you, is greater than the adversity that surrounds you. Keep working your gifts. God will open doors to share your time and talent. If you keep focusing on what you don't want, you'll keep getting what you don't want. Change what you're focusing on. In order to attain victory and cross the finish line of your vision; it takes focus, consistency, determination, and tenacity, to walk in your destiny. Manage your emotions, fine-tune your focus, and execute with purpose. Go for it and focus on it.

WHAT A TIME TO BE ALIVE

An African Proverb suggests, "There are two important dates in your life; the day you were born and the day you realize WHY you were born." The "Why" symbolizes that you have a purpose. Are you maximizing your purpose or allowing people and circumstances, to minimize your purpose? Yes, there will be challenges and setbacks, but when you know your purpose, nothing can keep you back for long. When you discover your WHY, you will find a WAY to bring the vision to fruition.

LIVE ON PURPOSE

You weren't born to merely exist. You were born to live with purpose, on purpose, and for a purpose because you have a dynamic purpose. When you're focused on taking care of your business, you don't have time to be in anybody else's. Your purpose for living, must light the cauldron of your motivation each day.

Each day you are blessed with 1,440 minutes and 86,400 seconds, in a span of 24 hours. The way you use your 24 hours, will open the door or lock you out of success.

Don't let time use you, but be proactive to use your time wisely or life will pass you by. Since you have been blessed with life, right now is the right time to revisit the goal and forge ahead into your future. Realize that the more time you spend looking backward, is the less time you have to move forward.

Shake yourself out of sadness, procrastination, and negative thinking. Begin to get excited about life and life will bring the excitement that you desire. The only person that can stop you, from living your best life is you. Your circumstances don't define you, they refine you. Use your time wisely, by creating your best life through the power of your thought life. Remind yourself, despite struggles and adversity that every setback is a set up for victory.

Despite what it looks like, this is still an exciting time to be alive. Don't give up and throw in the towel. Yesterday is gone and tomorrow is not promised. All that you have is right now. Get back in the race, stay focused, and surround yourself with goal-getters. Disconnect from dream killers and position yourself on the path to purpose.

I WAS BLIND, BUT NOW I SEE

Every year or so, I pay a visit to the optometrist to check my vision. I wear glasses because I struggle with seeing far distances, especially when driving at night. During a visit, the optometrist will examine my sight, through routine exams, in order so that I can see clearly.

Various trials, challenges, and tribulations have tried to blur your vision. In spite of it all, The Great Physician has given you foresight, insight, and hindsight to overcome every obstacle within your sight and push you onward to victory.

Helen Keller, who overcame adverse obstacles, became the first deaf-blind person to earn a Bachelor of Arts degree. She expressed, "The only thing worse than being blind, is having sight but no vision."

Proverbs 29:18 reminds us that "Without a vision, the people perish." Your natural sight can only take you so far, but vision can push you further. Sight is of the eyes, vision derives from the mind and heart.

Your vision keeps you alive, gives you purpose, and unlocks the door to your destiny. Walk in your vision and provision will become the byproduct of it.

Below are four ways to bring your vision to fruition and see your goals clearer than ever before:

1. Fine Tune Your Focus.

Your level of focus, has everything to do with stagnation or progression in life. Don't take detours to destruction, via distractions. Vision gives you clear direction, to avoid detours and distractions altogether. Stay focused. When you're focused, you can still have clear vision on a cloudy day. This is your time to focus, plan, and execute your vision to perfection. Great opportunities await.

2. Be Blind To The Past.

You know you're making progression, when everything around you is trying to stop you, from moving to the next level. Sometimes it's the past that tries to creep into your mindset to thwart your progress. In spite of it all, you have to blast past your past. Philippians 3:13 reminds us, to "Forget those things which are behind and reach forward, to those things which are ahead." The past is a prison, but the future is freedom. Begin to breakthrough and walk in freedom, by presently breaking away from your past. Don't beat yourself up over something you can't change. It's over. Get up and move your life forward.

3. 3D Vision.

Recognize that you are Distinct, Distinguished, and Destined to overcome the odds. Begin to see beyond what you see. Begin to see beyond your circumstance. Start walking by faith, not by sight. When you walk by faith, you transition from natural sight to supernatural vision. Start surrounding yourself with people who have vision, because they can see in you what you don't see in yourself. How can the blind lead the blind? People with no vision, want you to be blind like them. Connect to people who have vision. Vision helps you to see life through a different lens.

4. Vision Births Provision.

When you're passionate about your purpose, it will ignite your vision. First your vision gets into your heart, your head, and then into your hands to create something great. Get away from negative people, who want to kill your dream and abort the vision that's within you. You're pregnant with purpose, promise, possibility, and potential. It's time to push that vision to another level and deliver your destiny. Get around people who are pro your vision, because that will be a springboard to ensuring provision. Your vision will take you, where God's provision will meet you.

CHAPTER 9

My Sister's Keeper

Real sisters don't compete, they collaborate.
They see the best in you and want the best for you.

W hat does it mean, to be your sister's keeper and why is that important? It seems to be a rather daunting task, to say the least. It's hard enough to be responsible for yourself, much less someone else. In a society that is inculcated, with a "me first and only" mentality, it takes transformation to think collectively and critically.

COLLABORATION OVER COMPETITION

Real Queens don't compete, they collaborate. Competition divides, but collaboration unites. You don't need to operate in a spirit of competition, but rather collaboration with your sister. Scripture suggests, "One can chase a thousand and two can put ten thousand to flight" (Deuteronomy 32:30). Imagine what a host of unified sisters can do,when they're on one accord. Now that's real girl power!

TOO UNIQUE, TO COMPETE

There are more than seven billion people, on this planet. It's unbelievably remarkable, that there isn't a second you, anywhere to be found. You can search high and low, far and wide, but God only created you to do the work that He ordained for you to complete. Don't waste your time, trying to compete. You are totally unique.

The enormity of God's call on your life, is so expansive, that the Psalmist declared, "I am fearfully and wonderfully made" (Psalm 139:14). Nobody can duplicate, imitate, or replicate your uniqueness. You are a once, in a lifetime phenomenon. You're too unique, to compete. Why are you competing with another woman for a man's affection? If he doesn't realize your value and worth, stop wasting your breath, time, and energy. Just walk away. There will never be another you. Just do, what you were created to do.

IT'S TIME TO LEAP

When you create purposeful partnerships with strong sisters, the gifting and anointing on your life, will cause each of your visions to leap. In Luke 1:41, Mary went to visit her cousin Elizabeth, after being told by an angel that she was highly favored and would conceive a son named Jesus. Upon her arrival, at the sound of her salutation, the Bible records "The baby leaped in Elizabeth's womb and she was filled with the Holy Ghost." At that time, Mary was pregnant with Jesus and Elizabeth was pregnant with John.

You know that you're connected to the right people,

when they cause your vision to leap. You have been crippled by enough people, who made you limp through life. Despite the opposition, this is the season where God is sending the right people with the right connections, to cause your vision to leap.

Just like Mary, when you walk in the room and begin to speak, your blessing is going to recognize you because of the favor on your life. You've been limping long enough, but God is healing you of everything that crippled you. This time you're going to be rejoicing and leaping, into the greatness that is on your life. It's time to leap into entrepreneurship. Leap into full-time ministry. Leap back into college to get your degree. Leap out of a bad relationship, that keeps you limping. Leap and don't look back.

MARY MARY

My *Dear Queen*, God is sending a Mary into your life, that

will cause your vision to leap. The favor on her, will leap on your life. She will instruct you, correct you, and speak favor over your life. She is your sister in the bond. She is not your competition. She is your collaboration. She is your prayer partner, a shoulder to lean on, and surrogate sister soldier. She will fight with you, not against you. The wrong ones hated on you, but the right ones will elevate you.

For every woman that was messy, God is sending you a Mary. God is sending you a strong sister, that will empower you and cause your vision to spring forth. God is redeeming the time and giving you double for your trouble. They meant it for evil, but God is turning it around for your good.

SISTER, SISTER

Dear Queen, sometimes you need another sister to confide in. When you face tough times, do you turn to your sister(s) and seek help, or are you too busy competing with them and isolating yourself in caves of calamity? True sisterhood goes beyond a sorority or blood, it's forged by a bond. In good and bad times, a real sister empowers you through circumstances.

We must start building each other and stop competing, against each other. You know how to put up your guard and cover your emotions very well. You know how to act like you have it all together. You could literally get an Oscar for your acting ability. You have learned those steps, like a hustle dance routine.

Do you know how to provide, protect, and truly empower your sister? Oftentimes, men struggle with being vulnerable, for the sake of not being seen as someone who is strong. One of the beautiful things about your femininity, is how you can express your vulnerability communicatively. Only a beautiful being designed like you, can express uncanny sensitivity while remaining strong. I will speak for the men and say, that we could learn from you. I'm sure that we can learn, that it's not about what makes us cry that defines us. It's about what we do after we dry our tears, that refines and empowers us. Pray for discernment and divine connections with sisters, who will strengthen you.

REAL SISTERS

To win in life, you need teammates, not opponents. The right teammates will collaborate with you, not compete against you. A real sister who has your back, will empower you to move forward. They see the best in you and want the best for you. A real sister will keep it real with you and correct you, in love. She will pray with you, encourage you, coach you, and bring out the champion in you. She knows your worth, because she recognizes her own. As a result, your success is hers, because you're in the fight together. A real sister won't smile in your face and stab you behind the back. She won't flirt with your boyfriend or husband, when you turn your back. She won't tell you to leave a good man, because she's jealous of your relationship. She respects herself enough to respect you.

PUT SOME "RESPECK" ON MY NAME

A real sister will put some "respeck" on your name. She won't tell you what people said about you, she will defend your character when you're not around. Proverbs 22:1 declares, "A good name is rather to be chosen than great riches, and loving favor rather than silver and gold." Fame and fortune is meaningless, if you have a bad name. At the end of the day, your name is all you have. God said, "I will make your name great" (Genesis 12:2). Oftentimes, we try to do with titles, what we can't do with our name. People name drop and try to connect themselves with the elite and "who's who" of society to upgrade their value, self-worth, and name. When you serve the Name above all names and remain humble, then He will increase your influence. When you lift His name, he will lift your name.

Respect is not given, it's earned. There is no respectability without responsibility. You can't act in any manner or say what you want and expect to be respected. You can't expect a man to respect you, if you won't respect yourself. Become what you seek to attract. If you keep saying all men are dogs, you'll keep attracting the ones who bark, bite, give you fleas, and flee your presence.

The journey to love and embracing your inner royalty, often goes through hurt, pain, and life's rough terrain. People have already decided how to approach you or have made up their mind not to, based on the way that you carry yourself. When you walk in grace, you will never become a disgrace. Always think about what you do or say, if you want people to "Put some respeck on your name."

SISTER SOLDIER

Now is the time, to link arms together with your sister, beyond ethnicity or background. As you are linked together, begin to fight the good fight of faith. In the spirit of Fannie Lou Hamer, many of us are "Sick and tired of being sick and tired. Nobody is free until everybody is free." Put on your spiritual war clothes, as mission minded soldiers to pray and act. There is work to be done and battles to be won. There are lives in need of rescue, from the fires of futility, and the ashes of anguish. It's time to uplift and elevate your brother's confidence, stabilize your sister's life, and enhance the lives of our young people.

In our communities, we are often like fingers that are divided, simply poking at problems. We are doing great things separately, but imagine what we can do cohesively and collectively.

The crippling effects, of the "Willie Lynch"

philosophy and "Post Traumatic Slave Syndrome," has kept us in a state of distrust of one another. It has kept us divided, rather than united. If we can ever bring our fingers together and become like a fist, we will see victory in our community. When we bring our gifts, assets, and resources together, then we will see transformative progression. When we are united, we can address drug abuse, poverty, education, incarceration, and mental health issues.

We have operated in disunity, division, and disorganization for far too long, by design. Scripture declares "A house divided against itself, cannot stand"(Mark 3:25). Our community has operated, being separated like fingers far too long. We are doing great things separately, but teamwork makes the dream work and we're stronger when we become like a fist. For 400 years, they have sought to keep us separated, because the oppressor understood the power of unity.

We will only be able to clean up our communities, uplift our brothers and sisters, stabilize our schools, reduce unemployment and incarceration, if we work together. It's true that "Coming together is a beginning, keeping together is progress, but working together is success."

When we come together like a fist, we can knockout violence. When we become like a fist, we can knockout poverty. We can knockout the high school dropout rate. We can knockout drug abuse. It's time to fight the good fight of faith.

It's time to work together to bring transformation, in our communities and express love to one another. Your power is in your purpose. Your strength is in your stability and your restoration is in your reconciliation. You are a lady of royalty. There is a Queen in you. Begin to walk, talk, act, and live like it. You are a lady of liberty, daughter of destiny, and one of God's divine DIVAS.

DIVAS

I define DIVAS as *Divinely Inspired Virtuous Accomplished Sisters*. DIVAS are entrepreneurs, nurses, doctors, lawyers, teachers, beauticians, domestic engineers, and all around leaders. You can't deny the power of a Queen, especially in a society that is ever-changing. Women are leaders in business, medicine, technology, entertainment, and education.

Real DIVAS know the value that they possess and as a result, create empowering standards to live by daily. I often tell Queens, "Always keep your standards, higher than your heels." People will treat you, according to the standards that you set and put into practice for yourself. The standards that you set, will elicit the respect that you receive, or lack thereof. It's more than lip service, it has to be expressed in your lifestyle.

As you have read many themes throughout this book, hopefully you have begun to adopt a new mindset in the process. This is your greatest opportunity to live, love, and lift your life to a new level.

DIVAS, when a man sees you investing in yourself, he will be intrigued about investing in you. Don't get it twisted, I'm not referring to what he can buy you. I'm speaking to the value, that he can add to you. No number can add or multiply, exponentially on its own. It needs something of equal or greater value, to affect the sum of its substance. The right person will be an asset to you and add to your value. When you meet the right one, you're either going to be ready or trying to get ready. If you stay ready, you won't have to get ready.

A DIVA realizes that her personality and presence as a woman, supersedes her pulchritude and outward adornment. She understands her value on the inside, which permeates who she is on the outside. A woman's personality and presence, should be like potpourri to a room. More than beauty, her attitude should be a fragrance, not an odor.

Don't let a beautiful face, be ruined by an ugly attitude. Personally, I'm not so much concerned about a woman's color and curves, as I am the content of her character. When you can get both, that's a dynamic synergy.

In the movies, music, and relationship conversation, we always hear about love at first sight. I don't believe in love at first sight, I believe in like and lust at first sight. Beyond attraction, you can't truly love someone that you don't know. Take the time to go through the seasons with a person. Yes, Spring, Summer, Winter, and Fall. People change with the seasons, so pay attention to the changes.

One of the biggest mistakes that you can make is to settle, just to say you have somebody. Sometimes the one you're with, is not the one God wants. Ask yourself, "If I join forces with this person, will I be in the red or the black? Are they an asset to me or a liability for me?"

As you invest in yourself, begin to pamper and keep yourself up. Enhance yourself holistically. There's nothing like a Queen, who keeps a manicure/pedicure, goes to MAC to do her makeup (not heavy), and she can make some mean mac and cheese.

AM I MY SISTER'S KEEPER?

There are three imperative questions, denoted in the book of Genesis. The first is presented, in the Garden of Eden, after Adam and Eve sinned against God. They sinned by eating, from the tree of the knowledge of good and evil. As a result, they hid (Genesis 3:6-12). God asked Adam, "Where are you?" It's a question that provokes one, who has lost direction. It's interesting, that God never asked Eve the question. It's a question, that God is continually asking us today. Where are you in life? Where are you, in our communities? Where are you, in the lives of children and families? The question should cause you to ask yourself, "Where am I?" We see the struggles that we're facing, but confused as to how we can overcome it, wandering aimlessly. Fear has caused us to go into hiding. We have hidden our gifts, power, intellectuality, ability. Much like Adam we point the blame, at everyone and everything else, except ourselves. We have gone into hiding, because we have not followed the direction of God.

The second question in Genesis 4:6, God asks Cain, "Why are you angry?" Oftentimes as individuals, we are angry and don't know why. Filled with rage, because we refuse to confront our issues. Bitterness, strife, and anger will hurt you long term. Unbridled anger, is one action away from danger. We must exercise self-control, or we will harm others and ourselves in the process.

The third question, has become one of the most powerful pronouncements, since the beginning of time. The question is, "Am I My Brother's Keeper?" For this chapter we can interchangeably ask the question, "Am I *My Sister's Keeper?*" This is the first statement recorded in scripture, of a human being asking God a question. The story of Cain and Abel, found in Genesis 4:1-12, is a familiar story. Yet it is entrenched in anger, competition, drama, envy, jealousy, rage, and ultimately murder.

The Bible doesn't express, how effective Adam and Eve were as parents. We don't know what family vacations, that Mr. Adam and Mrs. Eve, took their beloved children on. However, we do know, within this cannon of scripture, that Cain and Abel were not reared as lazy boys. These children were born after the fall of mankind, as sin entered into the world, because of the disobedience of their parents.

As a result, Adam and Eve were sent out of the garden, to work the ground from which they were created. They once relished in the pristine paradise, of the Garden of Eden. Yet, were now cultivating a garden, that produced weeds, around the seeds and crops that were planted. It's evident that Cain and Abel, didn't grow up with a "silver spoon" in their mouths. These boys were tending the fields, cattle, and tilling the ground. They were engaged in hard labor, through an agrarian way of life.

FAMILY MATTERS

The first three chapters of Genesis, sets the stage for human history and the fourth chapter begins to play it out. The fourth chapter introduces the first childbirth, the first formal worship, the first division of labor, the first signs of culture, and ultimately the first murder.

In my study and analysis of this chapter, I always wondered, when did Cain turn on Abel? Was his anger against his brother, built up over time? Was it episodic or was his murder of Abel pre-meditated? Did Cain have a lapse in judgment and all of a sudden just snap? The people who betrayed you, turned on you a long time ago before their actions manifested into betrayal. They secretly hated you, long before they hurt you.

This particular story, has the makings of a reality TV show. It's *Scandal* and *How to Get Away with Murder*, all rolled into one. This story is a "made-for-TV drama" thriller series, that could possibly be called *The Adam's Family*. This family would make the Kardashians seem normal.

When it came time to present the offerings to God, Cain was not what you would call "a cheerful giver." His attitude towards the offering and his brother, was totally unethical. So, by the time Cain killed his brother, it was already "justified" because he destroyed him mentally, before he committed the act physically. Rather than strengthen his brother, Cain destroyed his brother. Rather than being compelled by Abel's worship, Cain competed for validation from God. This scandal has affected every corner of the world, throughout human history and continues to play out. Cain never got away with murder, because God cursed him for slaying Abel.

The resounding question is, "Are we our brother's and sister's keeper?" This question, continues to reverberate in our communities, as we face the conundrums of our world. You may have never been like Cain and killed someone, but you killed someone's character with your words. Your words were verbal triggers, that assassinated someone's self-esteem. You didn't kill anybody, but you thought about it. Who are the Abel's in your life, that you perpetrated against? Who did you enable negatively? I know that none of us are perfect and we have inflicted wounds on others, because of how we have been treated. Oftentimes we put others down, because no one lifted us up. However, we must not use the pain as an excuse to continue on the wrong path. The voices of slain brothers and sisters in the streets, are crying out through bloodshed.

The voices of those victimized by police brutality, cannot be silenced. The voices of sisters abused in homes, that should express love but embody hatred, are in need of help.

The voices of wayward young women, are screaming for their fathers and mothers. The voices of those who are addicted and conflicted, are crying out for freedom. No longer can we roll over and play dead. No longer can we hide our faces in the sands of our situations. No longer can we turn our back, on prevalent issues in our communities. We can't live in a state of denial, with a denigrated, desecrated, and destructive spirit of Cain. We must face issues with boldness, to bring reconciliation to struggling lives.

PRISON WITHOUT BARS

According to PrisonPolicy.org, 5 percent of the world's female population lives in the United States. The United States accounts for nearly 30 percent, of the world's incarcerated women. Since 1980, the number of women in prison has increased, at nearly double the rate for men. To add, America's female prison population has increased over 800 percent, in the last two decades.

Why is the female prison population skyrocketing? Without a doubt the pseudo war on drugs and related enforcement policies, have directly contributed to the increase in the number of women incarcerated. The targeting of black and brown communities, by design is another factor. However, there is a deeper concern as a vast majority of incarcerated women report a history of physical and sexual abuse, prior to being incarcerated. Many have reported that the abuse occurred when they were minors. As a result, many suffer from mental health issues, engage in risky behavior and abusive relationships, which often lead to a life of addiction and criminality.

Too often our sisters and brothers are locked away,

because no one ever unlocked their purpose. When many of our brothers should be at Morehouse, they are locked away in a prison house. Our sisters have untapped potential, but many are relegated to a state prison instead of Spelman. When many of our brothers and sisters, could aspire for higher education at Cornel and Yale, they find themselves confined to a prison cell.

According to the African American Policy Forum, black girls are suspended at a higher rate, than all other girls, including white and Latino boys. Sixty-seven percent of black girls reported feeling sad or hopeless, compared to 31 percent of white girls and 40 percent of Latinas. To further assert, single black women have the lowest net wealth of any group, with a median wealth of only $100. Fifty-five percent of black women have never been married, compared to 34 percent for white women. Much like their brothers, black and Hispanic girls are at or near the bottom level of reading and math scores. The gender specific risks, include being more likely to be victims of domestic violence, sex trafficking, and the juvenile justice system. The adverse issues affecting black women and girls, have been ignored far too long.

As we seek to save and build our brothers, we must not ignore the plight and promise of our sisters. We always talk about the broken lives, that need to be fixed. Let's not turn a blind eye, to the broken communities that many of our brothers and sisters come from, which need to be fixed as well. The adverse conditions that communities of color live in, compound the problems we face. Yes, our sisters are resilient, but we cannot be negligent to ignore their needs which call for remediation. Somebody dropped our sisters and refused to bandage their wounds. Will you be the Good Samaritan to lift someone's life? To be physically incarcerated is perplexing, in and of itself. However, to be psychologically incarcerated in a prison without bars, is even more tragic. Don't allow someone's abuse of you, to cause you to misuse your life. You will continue to live in the pain of your past, until you discover freedom from it. Bounce back from every setback and share your story, to strengthen someone's life.

ACCOUNTABILITY

From the beginning of time, it is clear that God places a high priority, on how we treat each other. You being your sister's keeper, extends past being someone's relative. It's about you being able to relate to sisters, who may not look like you or have your experience. Your love must grow deeper, because you are your sister's keeper.

The word used for "keeper" in Hebrew is *shamar.* This word means to guard, protect, support, and regard highly. Yet, the looming question today is "Are we responsible, for our sisters?" I believe God would respond with an emphatic "Yes, we are responsible for our sisters." Not only are we our sister's keeper, but we are also held accountable for our treatment of our brothers. We must not break and bash them, we must build them. In our communities, we used to look out for each other, now we look away from each other. We are accountable for one another. This accountability is beyond relational, it's communal and spiritual.

FILLING THE VOID

The issue of responsibility, still hits home to me and is personalized. If you were like me, you grew up in a single parent home. My mother, did her best in trying to navigate the role of mother and "father." When in actuality, no parent can ever play both roles. I do have to give mom her props though. She taught me, how to dribble a basketball and kick a football. Yes, she got game.

Prior to my parents divorce, my father was in the house for a period of time. However, when he was there, he wasn't there. Have I lost you? When he was present physically, he was absent mentally, relationally, and spiritually.

As a young boy, I witnessed and endured the absence of my father from our household. I was perplexed, being faced with abandonment and rejection. Imagine the scars left on a child's life, who is searching for identity in society without proper rearing. You can't help, but ask the questions: What did I do wrong, for you to leave? Am I not the son you wanted? Am I not worthy of love?

So, like many fatherless young men today, I looked for a father figure on the television screen. However, athletes, actors, and celebrities couldn't fill the void. I tried to cover the hurt by acting tough, because I was angry. I surrounded myself with friends, who were not always the right crowd to be around, which clouded my decision making. Sports became my outlet, through the game of basketball. I looked to Michael Jordan, as a "father figure" on television. I admired his perseverance, tenacity, and competitive drive. Yes, Air Jordan could soar beyond the stratosphere, yet the apex of his aerial artistry couldn't soothe my apathy, calm my fears, or wipe away the tears.

Maybe you have asked, "How can I be responsible, if I never saw it exemplified in a parent?" Now, as the father removes himself from the mother and the child's life, it leaves a feeling of rejection in their lives. As a result, children begin to appropriate abandonment in many forms, whether psychologically, emotionally, or spiritually.

Now, many begin to "act out" or rebel, because all they know is hurt. So, it begins to replicate in our relationships. The hurt manifests, through physical or verbal abuse, inadequacy, insecurity, and a lack of responsibility.

FORSAKEN BUT NOT FORGOTTEN

I can truly say, when my father left me, then the Lord lifted me up (Psalm 27:10). God is lifting you above your circumstances and previous experiences. We often place the caution tape around ourselves, that reads, "do not cross" because of past hurt. There are places in our lives that need remediation, because you and I are under construction. Don't allow your dusty past, to lead to a destructive future. Allow yourself the space to heal, in order to sweep out the areas that become stumbling blocks in your life.

It is to our advantage and the ultimate benefit of others, that we begin to open up ourselves. Just like me, you may have never experienced love from your earthly father. However, your Heavenly father is waiting with open arms, to embrace you with His perfect love. We must first open ourselves to God, to experience the magnanimity of His blessings. He has the power to lift you higher. You may have been forsaken, but God has not forgotten you. He will never leave or abandon you.

TRUE VALUE

Knowing your true value, means that you can't continue to engage in illegal, illicit, and self-destructive behaviors, which diminish your life. No longer can we destroy each other's lives, through violence and crime. No longer can we berate our brothers and reduce them to anything lower than a King. We cannot continue to demean our fellow sisters and call them anything but a Queen, or a child of God.

Now is the time, to improve the impoverished areas and facets of life. It begins with improving ourselves interpersonally, by recognizing our true value collectively.

FEMALE VS. WOMAN

Just because you have the outer makings, of what a female looks like, that doesn't make you a woman. Gender makes you female, but grandeur and character development qualifies you to be a woman. It takes character to be the Queen of quality, that you were created to be.

Womanhood is about more than having a female body, it's the mentality which outweighs your feminine physique. I repeat, gender is what makes you female, but character is what makes you a woman. It's significant to realize, that you can be a female and still not be a woman. Being born female doesn't make you a woman, any more than standing in a garage makes you a car. What separates you from the masses beyond your sultry smile, fit frame, or voluptuous physique?

SO YOU CALL YOURSELF A QUEEN?

A real Queen understands, that it's not about being knocked down, that defines her womanhood. It's what she does, after she's knocked down, that defines it. You never lose because you were knocked down. You only lose because you decided to stay down. Even if you have to crawl and cry, get back up and overcome the situation.

To the world you look ordinary, but on the inside you have extraordinary power and potential. Activate your purpose, power, and potential. Brush your shoulders off. Shake yourself and get back in the fight.

You may have been hit, but don't quit. Who are you, beyond what you possess? Who are you, beyond your recognition, notoriety, and success? The essence of your womanhood, has nothing to do with what you have attained. It has everything to do, with who you are and what you do, to inspire others as a Queen. You are your sister's keeper.

CHAPTER 10

Build Your Queendom

*To flourish, grow, and build your Queendom, you have to
release the liabilities and only retain those,
who are assets to your life.*

According to researchers and business analysts,
"2.9 million firms are majority-owned by women of color in
the United States. These firms employ 1.4 million people and
generate $226 billion in revenue annually." Indeed, women
are a force to be reckoned with as builders in business.

An entrepreneur can been described as someone who
jumps off a cliff and builds a plane on the way down, without
a parachute. Indeed there is risk and reward in business. As
indicated by 2018, there will be 100,000 new millionaires in
the U.S. Of the 100,000 millionaires, 56 percent won't have a

degree and 35 percent will work from home to build their empire. Will you be in that number? If so, how will you get there? What are you doing now, to position yourself for lucrative opportunities? How are you using your time and talent, to create the treasure you desire?

POWER AND EMPIRE

You have to recognize and realize, that to build your Queendom, you can't sit idle. You can't be a couch potato, wasting time watching TV or you will suffer from tunnel vision. Too many people are watching *Power*, but have none. They watch *Empire*, but won't build one. Building an empire is not about watching the season finale of a TV show. It's about putting in the hustle, sweat, and tears so that your work can show. It's the heart, hope, and hustle that presents new opportunities daily. Yesterday was a success, but what will you make of today?

I heard someone say, "Yesterday's home runs can't be placed on the scoreboard to win today's games." It's what you're doing today and right now, that makes the difference. To build an empire with power takes focus, desire, and precision. Building your empire and dreams, takes risk to reap the rewards.

Allow purpose to position you, on the path to prosperity. Building your empire is not about chasing money, it's about pursuing your purpose. When you pursue your purpose and work your gifts, money will chase you. You can't truly build a formidable empire, if you don't have a foundation. Take the time to recognize your value and gain greater knowledge of your true worth.

INVEST IN YOU

Begin to invest in yourself. Understand that your value is not determined by what you have, it's determined by who you are. Be careful of the people, who you place in your space. Your network, determines your net worth. To flourish, grow, and build your empire, you have to release the liabilities and retain only those who are assets to your life.

What do you have that money CAN'T buy? You are not truly rich or wealthy, until you possess what money can't buy. It doesn't matter if your business is booming. If you are bankrupt on the inside, your business will soon be bankrupt on the outside. A woman who builds her Queendom is not focused on getting a man, because she is working her plan. She is investing time in the permanent vision that God gave her, not in temporary relationships that will bankrupt her business.

Your King is a visionary, who sees the Queen qualities in you and makes an investment for your future. He will do more than pay for you, he will pray with and for you. A true Queen knows how to pray, encourage, and nurture the King in a man. Take the time to invest in yourself, nurture your growth, build your ideas, evaluate your relationships, feed your spirit, and you will be able to Build Your Queendom.

HANDS FREE

Don't allow your cell phone, to lock you out of developing a purpose driven relationship. We are living in a generation where people send likes and hearts online, but don't like themselves or allow love to flow from their hearts offline. Maybe we can be more loving, by logging off. These days, too many people hold their phones, instead of each other's hands. They scroll through social media and gaze at their screen, rather than into each other's eyes or at their smile.

Researches suggest that people who post countlessly about their relationship, are the main one's frustrated in it. Too often we allow associates and strangers, too much access into our lives and then wonder why good relationships end badly. Don't look to people to validate your relationship, with likes and comments. There are a lot of people who secretly hate you and publicly "like" you. Many people are not happy about your success. They are happy when you're sad and sad when you're happy. Never judge your relationship, by what other people are saying and doing. You're not in a relationship with them.

You will empower your relationship, when you power down your phone. If you're commenting more than communicating or posting more than investing in each other, then a sweet relationship will turn sour. Find balance, so you don't take them for granted. What you fail to appreciate, someone else will. Don't let your cell phone, become a prison. Use technology as a tool, so it won't become a handcuff.

SOCIAL MEDIA MOVEMENT

Learn how to leverage social media, beyond snapping selfies

and exposing your body. Create a social media movement. Use it to expose your business to the world. Understand branding and business. What you don't promote, doesn't exist to the world because you failed to expose it. Step out, launch out, and promote your greatness. Somebody is waiting for you to do it. When you leverage social media and build an organic following, you can literally be everywhere and in one place at the same time.

BUILD YOUR BRAND

What is the message that you desire, to convey to the world? Is that communicated through your words and images? Believe it or not, you are a brand. You are a billboard and people decide whether to invest in you or hide from you, based on your messaging. Your smile is your best business card. Never let your attitude or approach, be a reproach. Create the narrative by how you convey your story and connect it to your business.

It's never too early to build your business and brand, for the future. For the best way to predict your future, is to create it. In order to create it, you can't be afraid to dream big. If your dreams are affordable, then you're not dreaming big enough. Don't allow fear to place limitations on your dreams. Fear will paralyze you, but faith will mobilize you. The belief that you can do it, has to be greater than negative thoughts or doubt from others who think you can't. Let success mute your critics.

You can't be afraid to take the next step. Sometimes we are between a job and a dream. When you leave your job, come home and work on your dream. Work until your dream becomes your job. Don't stop by the mall. You have enough clothes, shoes, and bags. Don't go to the bar. Maintain your mental sobriety. You need inspiration, not intoxication. Go home and create your vision. Don't sleep on your vision.

You're not tired, you're just uninspired. Look deep within and will yourself to make it happen. Your "I will" is greater than your IQ. Don't allow your mindset and feelings to inhibit your dreams. Set goals and create action steps for progress.

VISION FOR VICTORY

Don't get bored with your vision, create a vision board. When you see where you want to be, you can seize the opportunity. Create your vision for victory. Find an accountability partner, who will challenge you to dig deeper and work harder. Invest in yourself and you will reap the benefits of your hard work. Nothing worth working for comes easy, that's why it's called hard work. However, if you love what you do, then your hard work will become easier.

WHAT'S YOUR WHY?

Discovering your purpose, is the key that unlocks the door

to passion and success. As I mentioned in chapter eight, "There are two important dates in your life; the day you were born and the day you realize WHY you were born." Have you discovered your WHY for living? Beyond just a million dollars, a fancy car, burgeoning career, fame, a spouse, two kids and a house. Billions of people are existing on this planet. Will you be the one to maximize the moment and begin maximizing your purpose? The discovery of purpose, is the antidote to the ills of life. Yes, there will be challenges and setbacks, but when you know your purpose it can't keep you back. When you discover your WHY, you will find a WAY to bring the vision to fruition.

I'd like to take that point further, because it's not the day that you became a business owner that's most important. It is the day you realize WHY you became a business owner, that is even more momentous.

Purpose gives you vision and vision puts you in

position to win, by pursuing your passion with persistence.

When you know your purpose, you can see a bright day in

a dark moment. Your most challenging setback, can become

a platform that launches your greatest comeback.

When I was at my lowest point, receiving

chemotherapy and radiation for two years. I had to trust

God, believe against all odds, and transform my mindset

for victory. I had to find the CAN in cancer, in order to

become an overcomer. Don't lose hope. Don't give up. Keep

believing and expecting that things will work out. Faith gives

you hope. Hope gives you strength and that strength will

sustain you, on your journey to success.

BLOOM WHERE YOU'RE PLANTED

Tupac Shakur, the rhetorical genius and rapper

extraordinaire, declared, "Be the rose that grows from

concrete." The tests, trials, and thorns of life are designed to be a breaking point that breaks you down. In the midst of it, you must breakthrough.

Begin to aim higher, push further, dream bigger, reach deeper, and stay rooted in God's Word to ignite your faith. Your life may have been planted in a negative environment or situation, yet you must begin to think positive in the midst of negativity. A changed situation is a byproduct of a changed mindset. Use the resources, ingenuity, and God-given gifts within you, to bloom where you have been planted.

GROW THROUGH IT

You are a rose, despite the thorns of life that seek to damage your petals of peace. Don't allow the weeds of worry, to choke the seeds of strength in your spirit. Make sure that what is planted in your mind, ears, eyes, and spirit will ensure your progress. You may have been hurt, stepped on, or knocked down but don't stay down. Get back up, brush your shoulders off and get back in the fight. Queen, straighten your crown. You were not built to breakdown. You were built to breakthrough. Grow through every adversity and obstacle.

FROM LOCAL TO GLOBAL

You're in a specific place and region for this season. Transform your world where you are. Begin to build your dream, right where you are and bloom where you have been planted. Start LOCAL and take it GLOBAL. You don't need a million dollars, to make your dream work. All you need, is a million dollar idea. Don't waste time waiting for a handout and a hookup.

If no one will give you an opportunity, then create your own. Work your gifts, stay on the path of purpose, and surround yourself with purpose driven people. God will give the increase.

MAKE ROOM TO BLOOM

To begin blooming, you have to keep pruning if you intend on growing. In order to bloom, you have to make room. There are some things that you have to cut away and get rid of to be effective. Growth brings with it growing pains, because change is uncomfortable. Sometimes it hurts to break away from bad habits and things you like to do, but know they aren't any good for you. Life is not fair and life will have pain. It's either the pain of discipline or the pain of consequence, your choice.

The pain of discipline comes from doing what you don't want to do, yet focusing on the task, with an end result in mind. The pain of consequence comes from not doing what you were supposed to do and suffering as a result. In order to grow and get better, you have to continually work to do it. There is no growth, without self-reflection and personal analysis. Self-development, spiritual wisdom, sound direction, and awareness of purpose are integral ingredients to foster your growth for the next level. Dig deep within the soil of your soul, to plant strength and reap a harvest of hope.

STOP BEING A CHICKEN

Are you a chicken or an eagle? Now, I'm not calling you a chicken. I'm just asking you a question. You're an eagle and you're right on the edge of greatness. I'm writing to push you over the edge, so you can spread your wings and soar into success. You're right on the edge of greatness. You can't be afraid to leap, spread your eagles wings, and soar to success.

In life you will either be a chicken or an eagle, worrier or warrior, whiner or a winner, chump or champion. You will either be broke or talk about those who have money. Which one are you? Who will you be? Many times what we become, is predicated on who and what we surround ourselves with daily. Are the people around you, adding to you or subtracting from you?

I'm a living witness that you can't get in the RIGHT places, if you're hanging with the WRONG people. Surround yourself with goal-getters and achievers, NOT dream killers. Some folks are sick about your success, hate your happiness, and envy your elevation. Move forward anyway. Make them sick and keep succeeding. Let them hate and the love you show will keep you happy. While they envy you, use your haters as elevators to go higher. Your enemies fail to realize, that if they would just celebrate instead of hate, then maybe they could participate.

MIND YOUR BUSINESS

When you're productively growing, handling, and taking care of your business, you won't have to put your nose in somebody else's business. On the contrary, if you bring everybody into your business, it will eventually go out of business. Learn how to keep some things to yourself. Stop telling everybody your next move. Breaking news alert: "Everybody is not happy about your success." Stop looking for people, who secretly hate you to openly applaud you. There are some people who don't want you to better yourself, because they can't handle a better you. Don't divulge every move or project, you're "about" to work on or release. Just move in silence, get the job done, and let your success make noise.

YOU NEED TO CUT IT

Some relationships need to be cut, so other things in your life can grow. Some things will grow incorrectly, unless they are cut properly and there are other things that won't grow at all until they are cut. The excuses you make need to be cut. The negative self-talk needs to be cut. Bad associations and unfruitful relationships need to be cut.

God will close the door on relationships that are worthless, because you're worth so much more. Don't go back and get what God delivered you from. If you really knew who you were, the anointing and purpose on your life, then you would introspectively evaluate and cut away things that hinder you. The price of your value is way too high, you need to cut it.

EAGLE EYE

Begin to surround yourself with eagles, NOT chickens. Eagles are visionaries. They develop concepts, embark on their goals, and dream big. They don't have time to talk about individuals, because they are developing ideas. They turn ideas into income. They transform contacts into contracts. You know you're in the presence of eagles, when they want to see you grow. Eagles don't sit on you, after your ideas have hatched. They don't want to clip your wings, rather they desire to teach you how to soar. Eagle eyed individuals have keen vision, to see in you what you may not see in yourself. They are not jealous of the jewels in you or desire to steal your joy. They won't fight you, but will fight for you. They stand in faith with you.

PRAY OR PREY?

Empowered eagles do not PREY on you, they PRAY for you. Chickens disguised as eagles, are like wolves in sheep's clothing. They sit on the sidelines expecting your demise. The only time they clap, is when they think you lost or will quit. People who are comfortable in themselves and know who they are, can celebrate the success of others. Eagle type individuals want you to grow, but chickens will stunt your growth.

Both birds have wings, but only eagles can soar. Chicken type people spend more time clucking and gossiping, than they do working. They waste time pecking at their problems, instead of being proactive to solve those problems. Personally, I don't have anything against chickens I had some for dinner yesterday. I just refuse to fly with them, because I was made to soar. Stop being a chicken. Stop being afraid to walk in your purpose. Stop being afraid, to break away from toxic relationships.

What will they say about you, if you did something different? They will say the same thing, when you were doing the same thing. Let them keep talking and you begin soaring. Refuse to be prey for the enemy. Pray and give yourself the green light, to move forward in freedom.

VISION FOR YOUR MISSION

In order to build your Queendom, you must possess an eagle eye. The eagle is a unique species. It symbolizes America's national emblem, to embody the spirit of freedom, liberty, and powerful. The eagle is a majestic bird to behold. If an eagle were to spread it's wings in your presence, it would measure nine feet from tip to tip.

Eagles have more than just sight, they have vision. As I indicated before, "If you have sight but no vision, then you're still blind." Sight is merely of the eyes, but vision comes from the heart. Eagles live on another level. They think on a greater level. Eagles communicate and process thoughts on another level. Eagles dream and build on another level. Eagles were built for high places. They were built to soar. They were built to withstand the storms of life. When the storm comes and other birds fly away to seek shelter, the eagle flies into the storm and uses it to soar higher.

You were not built to break under pressure. The pressure that you endure is making a diamond out of you. The strength you have within, will cause you to soar through the storm. Chickens are intimidated by eagles, but eagles are inspired by other eagles.

BIRDS OF A FEATHER, FLOCK TOGETHER

Even an eagle can teach us, how to overcome obstacles. Below are three things that eagles do, to soar above their situation:

1. Eagles Soar Alone.

Eagles soar at a high altitude. No other bird goes to the height of an eagle. If you're an eagle, start hanging with eagles. If everybody in your circle is clucking, crying, and complaining. Change it or you will never experience the ability, to soar into the stratosphere of success.

2. Eagles Have Strong Vision.

You need 3D vision, because you're distinct, destined, and delivered. Maintain a vision and remain focused, no matter the obstacle and you will succeed. It's not enough to have goals, you have to implement an action plan. Provision is a byproduct, of those who work their vision.

3. Eagles Soar Above Their Situation.

They use the negative positively, by gaining momentum in the storm. While everyone else is hiding, the eagle is yet rising. When the storm comes and other birds run for shelter, the eagle flies into the storm and uses it, to soar to higher heights. You know you're an eagle when the storm that should have killed you, wound up lifting you higher.

Spread your **W.I.N.G.S.**

Walk in **W**isdom…

Be **I**nspired…

Discover **N**ewness of Life…

Use your God-given **G**ifts…

Because God made you to be **S**pecial…

WHAT'S IN YOUR TOOLBOX?

God placed something inside of YOU, that the world needs. It's time for you to discover it and use it. Follow purpose, not money. When you follow purpose, money will follow you. Don't see money as the goal, it's only a byproduct of reaching the goal. The resources and gifts that you possess within, are enough to win and build your Queendom. Your gifts, skills, and abilities are the tools needed to bring your vision to fruition. What are you doing, with the tools in your box? Are you using them to build or break somebody down? Are you using them to hurt and harm, or to help and heal?

What do you have in your toolbox? You already have everything you need, because it resides inside of you. Now is your time to reach for it and use it. Build your Queendom by using the tools in your box. You will see that you have a **lightbulb**, to illuminate minds. You have **tape**, to piece together a life that may be tattered and torn. There is a **ruler** to measure your growth and progress, by gaining wisdom through Christ being the ruler of your life. In your toolbox is a **screwdriver**, to tighten up any loose ends, make revisions, adjustments, and turn lives around.

Are you looking in your toolbox? You will notice that you have a **hammer** of hope to breakdown barriers. Break down the barriers of misogyny, sexism, unequal pay, and racism.

In your toolbox are **nails** of knowledge, being driven into every goal, vision, and idea with the hammer of hope as a reminder to hold fast to your dreams. Remember, Jesus took the nails in His hands for you, to save you. The greatest love equation is 3 nails + 1 cross = 4 given.

Your toolbox has **glue** to ensure that you stick to the goal, plan, and objective to overcome. Remain committed to adhere to the adhesive. Come what may, keep holding tight and don't let go. Stay glued to the goal.

You have a pair of **scissors** to trim the rough edges of life. Cut away the fringes of failure and insecurity. For true growth to take place, some things have to be cut away.

What else is in your toolbox? A **flashlight** of faith, to bring substance to every shadow, light to every dark place, provide and point others to the path of purpose, prosperity, and peace.

You have **goggles** and **glasses**, to adjust your vision and see beyond what you see. If you can see the opportunity, then you can seize it.

You have a **paintbrush** to provide a spectrum of colors, by brightening the dark and desolate places in our communities.

To build your Queendom, use your **rope** of hope. Reach for those who are slipping away and pull them out of the cracks, in order to save their life from despair and dismay.

TOOLS, TALENTS, TREASURE

You are a builder, teacher, motivator to use what is in your toolbox and transform minds to think outside of the box. Use the gifts that God gave you. Use your smile, use your voice, your talent, and your education. Use your wisdom, use your substance, use your creativity, and your cognitive ability to inspire many.

Stop looking around for what you already have, it's in you. Our children need you, our schools need you, our communities needs you. Reach into your toolbox and pick up the baton, pick up your dream, pick up your gift, pick up your vision, and build a legacy for your children's children. You are the builder and architect of your life.

The world is waiting on you to open the business, recreation center, dance studio, school, mentoring program and outlets of opportunity that will empower communities. Why are you procrastinating and waiting? Now is the time.

Believe in what God placed in you. Use your tools, talents, and treasure to bring your vision to fruition. Be the CEO of your life and build your Queendom.

INVEST IN YOU

If you don't take the time to invest in yourself, who else will? Before proceeding to the next chapter, take a little time to be introspective and chart your goals and qualities.

So far, what are three principles that you have learned from the book and can apply to your life?

1.

2.

3.

What are your gifts and talents?

What strengths do you possess?

List several revenue streams that you can create.
(Example: writing a book, opening business, web design)

List three goal oriented people, who can help you to
maximize your potential. What skills do they possess?

1.

2.

3.

Your words create your world. Create three positive affirmations to confess over your life each day.

1.

2.

3.

Only 5 percent of people set goals. Out of those who set goals, 95 percent achieve the goals they set. Write five goals that you aspire to accomplish, in the next five months. Include your action plan for each goal.

<u>Goal</u>   <u>Action Plan</u>

1.

2.

3.

4.

5.

The average millionaire reads thirty books per year. List the books that you will read, to serve as food for your soul.

Psychologists suggest, it takes 21 days to break a habit. List the habits that you will break and the steps you will take to break them.

CHAPTER 11

Wear Your Crown

Wearing a crown doesn't make you a Queen. It's the qualities you exude, which qualify you to wear it.

You can't put a crown on a clown and expect them to act in a royal manner. What is on the clown, is a direct reflection of what is in the clown. The mindset of an individual, dictates how they will portray themselves. A crown is reserved for a special type of woman. She is not a Queen because she wears a crown. She was already a Queen before she wore it, because her mindset and actions, qualified her to wear it.

SWAG

A woman who exemplifies character, quality, and substance

is a Queen. She has style and a sophisticated swag. Her SWAG symbolizes *Someone Who Achieves Greatness*. She doesn't wait for a handout or a hookup. She uses the power in her mind and hands, to create opportunities for herself and others. Now that's real SWAG!

DELIVER ME FROM CLOWNS

We have seen a clown epidemic in America, where it seems as if society has turned into a circus. McDonald's, the fast food restaurant chain, gave Ronald McDonald a reprieve. It came as a result of the many creepy clowns, who were intimidating people throughout communities in America. You know, it's one thing to see clowns at the circus. It's another thing, to see clowns wandering in your community.

Don't subject yourself to relationship circus type antics, where people are juggling your emotions or causing you to flip out. You are not Pinocchio, stop allowing people to pull your strings and control you. Your prayer should be, "Lord deliver me from clowns." The destiny, purpose, and anointing that's on your life, is too important for you to waste it by clowning around.

NO CROSS, NO CROWN

The adversity that you have endured, in order to overcome, has qualified you to wear a crown. God doesn't call qualified people. He qualifies the people that He calls. You are approved. You are qualified. They doubted you, but God promoted you. They abused you, but God still used you. They left you for dead, but you're living through dying places. Don't tell me that your life doesn't have value. Look at what you have made it through. Some people gave up. Other people quit and many died, from what you overcame. What they thought would kill you, God used it to build you. Cancer made me cry, but it didn't make me quit.

The suffering you're experiencing, won't compare to the blessing you will be receiving. Don't give up, keep moving forward. The Apostle Paul encouraged us, in Romans 8:18, "For I reckon that the sufferings of this present time are not worthy to be compared, with the glory which shall be revealed in us." There will be glory after your situation, because it's being used as a vehicle to get to your destination.

Be encouraged in knowing that your cross crisis, is only a setup for the crown you will receive. Wearing a crown doesn't make you a Queen. It's the qualities that you exude, which qualify you to wear it. Heavy is the head that wears the crown, only when you think too much of yourself. There is no need to be conceited, if you remain confident. Believe in yourself. Confidence empowers you to win, before the race begins. False humility and conceit are too extreme, but confidence provides the right balance. Real Queens can walk boldly in who they are, without arrogance or insecurity.

It takes a Queen to endure the fire, come out as pure gold, and smell as angelic as *Thierry Mugler*. When you grow through and endure the cross, you become qualified to wear your crown.

QUEEN OF QUALITY

A Queen of quality, is the type to chase her purpose and plan, not a man. She isn't so thirsty for love, that anybody can quench it. She knows her value, loves herself, and becomes a magnet for love. She's not needy, she's needed. When you love yourself, you don't just settle for anything. You realize that God will give you the best of everything.

If they don't recognize your value, that's their loss. Don't beg anyone to see, what they choose to remain blind to. The right one will see and celebrate your value. *Dear Queen* take comfort in knowing, that your King will find you and complement your life. He won't just *compliment* you with flattering remarks, on your outer appearance. He will *complement* your inner vision and attributes, as a companion on the road to destiny. Don't look for somebody to complete you, God does that. You will remain incomplete, by looking for people to complete you. Take it out of their hands and put it in God's hands. He has the perfect person for you, that's perfect for you. Embrace who you are. You're the right type, so prepare for your prototype.

OWN IT

Recently, I spoke to hundreds of beautiful and successful ladies, during my seminar entitled, "No More Drama." The seminar encouraged women to love themselves, know their worth, and heal from broken relationships. During the seminar, I expressed that you have to own it, in order to heal from it. As a result, you will be able to make transitions for transformation to live your best life. Own the pain that you caused. Own the choices you have made and the mistakes of allowing people to mistreat you. The remedy comes, when you decide to confront the malady that caused it. If you don't shape your world, someone else will shape it for you. If you don't love yourself, someone will show you how to hate yourself. You are not a doormat, stop letting people walk all over you. Be assertive and take ownership, by being the CEO of your life. As a result, you may have to hire and fire certain people. It's not personal, it's just business. Evaluate, promote, and terminate in order to make your life work.

FORGIVE TO LIVE

You can't really live, until you forgive. How can you love again, if you haven't forgiven? When you forgive, it releases you to love again, despite the hurt and pain. Forgive those who have hurt you and forgive yourself, for allowing them to mistreat you. Forgiveness is never easy, but it's worth it in order to free yourself, from being held captive to the past. If you remain bitter, it will continue to break you down. You will never experience breakthrough, until it begins within you.

For many people in society, the greatest enemy is the "inner-me." They sabotage themselves with bad thoughts and decisions, that wreck their lives. You can't operate your life based on emotions. Your emotions will wreck your life. Whatever or whoever is holding you back, let it go so you can grow and more forward. There is no doubt, that you and I have been hurt and disappointed at times in life. Those were chapters in our lives, but it doesn't have to be the way that our story ends. A few bad chapters, doesn't define the story of your life. It's not what you go through, that makes your experiences significant. It's how you handle what you go through, that determines your strength.

GROW through the painful process and emerge with

greater power! Overcome being bitter, by pressing forward to become better. There is sagacity, strength, and an undying will within you, to win at all costs. Dig deep within the recesses of your soul and push ahead, by any means necessary. You must forgive, in order to live your best life. There are certain things, that you have to let go, in order for your life to flourish and grow. Sometimes there is isolation and separation, prior to your elevation. Rid yourself of toxic relationships and negativity, that are detrimental to your journey.

EVERYBODY CAN'T GO

You can't take everybody with you, on your journey to destiny. If I was driving a two-door *Lamborghini Murciélago*, why would I try to cram ten people into it? It just won't work. The same concept applies to life. You can't take everybody with you. It's not personal, it's just based on principle. Your purpose, is more important than pleasing people. If God is pleased with you, it doesn't matter if people aren't. Don't try to fit people from your past or present, into your future. Own the moment and make the adjustments.

Don't beg anybody to recognize your value. Your value doesn't decrease, based on someone's inability to see it. Some people will never SEE your value, because they are BLIND to their own. Realize and recognize that what you have is good enough. Who you are is great enough. Where you're going, is worth working hard enough to get there. Everybody gets their time to shine and moment to own it. Don't miss your opportunity.

MAXIMIZE THE MOMENT

If you lean to your own understanding, you will fall. Trust God through the process and you will make greater progress. Get up, launch out, and rise to the occasion. Stretch your faith, expand your mind, and dream bigger. Don't wait on anybody to create opportunities for you, create your own. No need to be needy and clingy, stand on your own two feet. Maximize every moment and own it.

Own your greatness. Own your beauty. Own your wisdom. Own your mistakes. Own your charisma. Own your self-worth. Own it and get stronger through it. Don't become bitter, because of what you've been through. Be better as a result of enduring it and coming out. Dare to be different. Don't follow the crowd. March to the beat of your own drum. You can't be imitated, replicated, or duplicated. Be uniquely you. Let your love and light shine through.

NOT YET

On a particular occasion, I spoke at a youth conference, promoting financial literacy and personal wealth. After my speech, one of the youngest attendees, approached me. As the little boy ran to me, he gave me a high five and said, "I want your shoes." I laughed, realizing that it would take him years, to grow into my size 12 shoes. I sarcastically said, "You don't want my shoes little bro, you've got the money to buy your own." He replied, "I can't buy your shoes right now, because I'm not a millionaire yet."

In the boy's precociousness and youthful glee, he didn't realize what he said was absolutely profound. His energy, comedy, and honesty, teaches us a lesson. Notice, the boy never said, he's not a millionaire. He also didn't assert, that he would never become a millionaire. However, the boy closed his sentence with the word, "yet."

The word "yet" speaks to what he believes, will be achieved, in spite of where he is right now. The word "yet" is only three letters, but it's packaged with power. Your words have power. Your words create your world. You have to recognize and realize, that your NOT YET, is greater than your right now!

The words "not yet" can be defined, as a future existing reality that presently hasn't happened. Can you see into the future, despite your present situation? You don't need BIG faith. Just have faith, the size of a mustard seed. Maintain that faith and vision, to perceive that nothing is impossible to achieve. Where you are now, is not where you will always be. You're going higher and farther, than you have ever been.

The greatest wisdom, is not always contained in a quote from Plato, Aristotle, Dr. King, T.D. Jakes, Iyanla Vanzant, Dr. Phil, Oprah Winfrey, Joel Osteen, Steve Harvey, or even Yours Truly. Sometimes the greatest wisdom, comes from the heart of a child!

If a little boy can say, that he hasn't achieved it yet, then why are you giving up at your age? Whatever age or stage, that you are in life, don't give up. Don't throw in the towel. Don't stop believing.

Begin to speak life to your situation, because your confession will eventually determine your possession. The term "not yet" doesn't mean it won't happen, it just conveys the fact, that it hasn't happened at this time. When a person asks, "Do you have it?" Don't say no, say "NOT YET!" It's not that you'll never be a millionaire, you're just not a millionaire YET. It's not that you won't achieve the dream, you just haven't achieved it YET. It's not that you won't get the scholarship, you just don't have it YET. Are you married? Not YET. Do you have the job? YOU don't have it YET. Do you have the promotion? You didn't receive it YET.

Remember the fact that your words, create your world. Your confession, will ultimately determine your possession. The power of "not yet" is the catalyst, that builds the bridge to the future, based on your confession. Begin to think positive, in every situation and see life through a new lens.

Think optimistically and work to achieve the dream proactively. It may not have happened yet, but believe the vision will come to fruition.

OBEY YOUR THIRST

Back in the 1990s, a very popular *Sprite* commercial for the soft drink soda, had a popular catch phrase. The narrator said, "Image is nothing, thirst is everything." The commercial culminated with the words, "Obey your thirst, *Sprite*."

In a new millennium, many millennials have adopted this philosophy to follow the trend, rather than to set a standard. I'm wondering, is what you're thirsting for, greater than the image of what you portray? Too many times people would rather look successful, than put in the work to actually be successful. The image you portray, is based on what you imagine in your mind. So the question becomes, what do you think about yourself? What is your truth? What is your narrative? Simply because, the image that you're reflecting, has everything to do with where you're going.

What are you thirsting for? See when you thirst for the wrong thing, you end up parched if not dehydrated. Too many people are thirsty for a date, instead of a degree. Thirsty to twerk, rather than to put in the work to make their dreams a reality. Thirsty for likes on Instagram, but dehydrated when it comes to showing love to the common woman or man. It's called Facebook for a reason, stop showing your behind.

How can you expect someone not to have an appetite, if all you bring to the table is meat? Don't call him "thirsty" if you're only parading your body as a beverage, that will quench it. Too many are thirsty to show their behind, rather than to put knowledge in their mind. Don't become so thirsty for love, that you just let anybody quench it. Allow God to fill you up with joy, love, and peace.

Oftentimes, we have become dehydrated and depleted, by negative relationships. We put our heart into a relationship and it wound up being toxic. It wound up depleting our strength and poisoning our spirit. Now we find ourselves, being thirsty for the wrong things.

The enemy will prey on your thirst and send the wrong person to distract you. The enemy understands, that you are a Proverbs 31 woman. The devil understands that you are pregnant with purpose, power, promise, possibility, and potential. As a consequence, he wants to abort your vision and the purpose on the inside of you. Despite the opposition, your connection determines your direction. When you are directly connected to God, then victory will be on the other side of the obstacle. You can say, "There will be glory after this" because your help comes from the Lord.

Matthew 5:6 affirms, "Those who hunger and thirst

after righteousness shall be filled." When you are thirsty for God, then He will fill your life with joy and peace. A man can't fill the space that only God can occupy. A new pair of heels or a designer bag, cannot fill the void in your life. Only God's Spirit, can fill the chasm and make you a reflection, of who He wants you to be.

GET IN FORMATION

I hope you don't mind, if I invite Queen B (that's Beyoncé if you live under a rock) into the chapter. See when you're thirsty for information, then we can all get IN FORMATION, to work together and reflect an image of empowerment.

When you have the information to get in formation, you can turn your lemons into lemonade. The bitter things in life will become better, because information produces transformation for productivity in your life.

WHAT ARE YOU THIRSTING FOR?

Are you thirsty enough to produce and not just purchase? To create and not just cash out at the mall? Stop thinking small and start thinking bigger. Do you see yourself achieving and becoming what you have imagined?

If you think little of yourself, you will do little for yourself. If you think much of yourself, you will do much for yourself and others. Growing up, I didn't think much of myself. My image was distorted. All I saw was the devastation of my diagnosis, with stage four cancer, rather than the revelation that the first three letters in cancer is CAN.

How much do you love yourself? Love for self frames the image for the life, that you will lead to impact others. Know your worth, begin to value yourself, and surround yourself with the type of people that value you. Get away from dream killers and get around GOAL getters.

THE MISSING INGREDIENT

We always talk about what's missing and broken in our communities, that we fail to recognize who is making a difference. My *Dear Queen*, you are NOT a statistic, you are a standout. You are not a detriment, you are determined. You are not a stereotype, you are a prototype for success. You are not a liability, you are an asset to your community.

REAL IMAGE

What image will you portray? What words will you begin to say? Real image is not about taking a selfie, with your name in lights. It's about being selfless enough, to pull someone out of the dark. Real image is not about how many followers, you have on social media. It's how you lead those who follow you. Real image is not about being on a reality show, it's about how much strength you can show, when no one else is watching. Real image is not about what you have, real image is about who you are.

Knowing who you are is based on coming into the awareness, that you are a divine daughter of the King of Kings. You will be dehydrated, if you only follow what *Sprite* said. The way that you portray yourself means everything. When you put your purpose first, you will never have to obey your thirst.

SORRY, I AIN'T SORRY

You don't owe anybody an apology, because you have decided to walk in greatness. Be a walking billboard for how God can turn a great mess into greatness. When they ask, "Who do you think you are?" Tell them you're a Queen. You are God's child. You are more than a conqueror. You are a daughter of destiny. Tell them what God says about you.

Don't apologize because you're beautiful inside and out. Don't make any apologies for your level of intelligence.

Stop reducing yourself, to make people feel comfortable with you. Their insecurity derives from their jealousy and feelings of inadequacy. You don't have to shrink yourself, to make others feel big. If they are offended by your greatness, that's their problem not yours. Refuse to reduce yourself and stoop to someone's level. Make them rise to your level and the standards you set.

I WOKE UP LIKE THIS

You don't have to ask for anyone's permission to be great. You were created for greatness. Yes, you woke up like this. Too many people have slept on your gifts, your worth, your vision, and intuition. God is getting ready to wake up the people who have slept on you, in order to showcase you. However, it will only happen when you wake up to the reality of who you truly are. Begin to walk in your unique purpose and gifts, that you were created to operate in.

You are delaying your progress, by waiting on people to accept you. You're wasting time, waiting on people to validate you. Some people will never acknowledge your gifts, because they don't even recognize their own. Wake up and stir up your gifts. Wake up the Queen within you. Be the Queen, that is driven to make your dream a reality. A Queen understands, that her hands will produce her harvest.

Proverbs 31:19 declares, "She layeth her hands to the spindle, and her hands hold the distaff." A Queen is a creator. She doesn't wait for a handout. She puts her hands out and creates something from nothing. She knows that her favor, will yield the fruit of her labor.

YOUR LABOR IS NOT IN VAIN

The labor that it takes to be successful, is worth working for to achieve. Effort, energy, and enthusiasm is the engine that propels you on the path towards purpose. Realize that your labor is not in vain. The harvest is indeed ripe, but the laborers are few. Do you have enough faith to walk the path alone, even when people doubt and give up on you? I'm a living witness, that your faith will carry you places, that your EYES can't SEE. In order to aspire higher, you have to believe and walk by faith.

LABOR PAINS

Life is filled with labor, which often brings about discomfort. You have to learn to be comfortable with being uncomfortable and become uncomfortable, with being comfortable. In other words, press past your comfort zone. Press toward the goal, in order to achieve the prize. Sometimes it requires you to push past the pain, in order to get there. Don't allow your feelings to cloud your focus. The prize is worth pressing for, to gain what you desire.

A mother knows that the process of childbirth is

arduous to say the least. In the pregnancy stages, a woman endures discomfort, many changes, contractions, and labor intensive pain to ultimately birth her child. In order for a mother to give birth naturally and deliver her child, she has to push.

My mother never had a caesarean section, much less pain when I was born. She told me that the doctor woke her up and said, "Your son is born." It was a pain free birth. So, I guess I can go on record saying that I never caused her any pain. To borrow a line from my cousin Prince, "I only wanted to see her, laughing in the purple rain."

On the contrary, some mothers endured pain which caused them to cry, scream, yell (or curse), and grip your hand. Delivering a baby, is the direct result of pushing past the pain. You too are pregnant with purpose. You have to push and deliver your destiny, by any means necessary.

PUSH

The same principles apply to your life. It's time to deliver and push out your dream. Push out your destiny and purpose, because you're pregnant with purpose. Don't let it die. Everything you need is ready to be birthed, but you have to push. You won't be fulfilled, until you push out that book. You will remain uncomfortable, until you manifest the entrepreneurial gift inside of you. Don't abort your vision. Don't let your dream die. Don't allow negativity to take up residence in your mind. Give birth to your goals and dreams. Work and PUSH, *Pray Until Something Happens.*

FROM LABOR TO FAVOR

In this season, God is moving you from LABOR to FAVOR. There are some goals, dreams, creative ideas, and business plans that you desire to birth and bring to fruition. However, it won't happen until you push through the obstacles.

There are some things, that you must stop laboring over and let go. Bad relationships and toxic connections, will drain you of your time, energy, and patience. Disconnect from negative people. Cease from laboring over those who are liabilities to your life, rather than assets for the uplifting of your life.

Don't let anyone or anything abort your purpose, possibilities, and potential. When you know *whose* you are and *who* you are, there is nothing that can stop you. When God is your Source, He will supply all of the resources that you need. Be comforted in knowing, that you will receive provision for your vision.

See opportunity in the midst of obstacles, because a setback is only a setup for your comeback. The love you share and the help you give is coming back to you. Your labor, will turn in your favor. Keep pushing, keep dreaming, and working. There is a great blessing coming. I can tell the size of your blessing, based on the battle that you're facing.

The bigger the battle, the BIGGER your blessing. Give birth to your gifts from within. If you put in the labor, God will release the favor. *Dear Queen*, wear your crown and refuse to dim your light. Keep sowing and growing. Your harvest is coming and your labor will produce favor.

A woman doesn't need a man to have favor, but a man needs a wife to find favor. Proverbs 18:22 explicitly tells us, "He who finds a wife, finds a good thing and receives FAVOR from the Lord." A Queen doesn't just become a wife, when she walks down the aisle in holy matrimony. A Queen has wife qualities, before she's presented with the ring. She's not preparing after a proposal. She's already ready, before she receives it. When a man finds a wife, his toil and labor will immediately transition to favor. Keep working on the vision that God gave you and the right man, will come searching for you. When a man finds his rib, he will breathe a lot easier. Finding what's missing, can become a man's greatest blessing. *Dear Queen*, don't forget to remember, you are the prize because of the favor on your life.

SLAY

The famous French fashion designer, Coco Chanel declared, "Always dress like you're going to see your worst enemy." In other words, she's telling you to "slay!"

I know you go to MAC and apply your makeup. You go to the salon and get your hair whipped, dipped, fried, dyed, and laid to the side. You get your mani and pedi. As the rapper Drake would say, "Oh you're fancy huh? Nail done, hair done, everything did." You style and profile in the mirror, as you put on your star spangled earrings.

Your lipstick is popping and your dress accents every curve, on your fine frame. You know you've got it going on, as you do your hair flip and step out of the house. Every man who sees you needs an oxygen mask, because your beauty takes his breath away. Naturally, the ladies admire you and the brothers want to be with you, because Queen you came to slay.

What would happen if we desired to slay spiritually, as we seek to do fashionably? In order to slay spiritually, you have to put on the whole armor of God. Everyday that you rise, there is a battle that you will face. Oftentimes, the battle is in your mind. You can't defeat the devil, unless you have the right weapons. Scripture declares, "For the weapons of our warfare are not carnal, but mighty through God to the pulling down of strong holds" (2 Corinthians 10:4). Only the weapon of God's Word, can give you the power to slay any attack of the enemy.

ARMED AND DANGEROUS

I'm sure your closet, contains some of the finest and fanciest clothes. Some years ago, I saw an MTV Cribs episode of Mariah Carey's home. In her walk in closet, she he had rows and rows of shoes in boxes. On the outside of those boxes, were pictures of each shoe. Any shoe you could think of, was in her closet from *Jimmy Choo* to *Manolo Blahnik*, from *Christian Louboutin* and *Salvatore Ferragamo*, to *Valentino Garavani*.

The shoes were quite exquisite and expensive, much like the ones you already own. I'm sure that your closet is similar to Mariah's, with pictures of your shoes on the outside of the boxes. Your bags and dresses are coordinated.

All of the accessories that you need, to accent your appearance and be DTI (Dressed To Impress) are within your grasp. When you get dressed, you just walk out of the door and slay everything moving. Just like you go through your closet full of items, you need to go into your prayer closet and intercede.

Beyond *Vera Wang, Jimmy Choo, Louis Vuitton, and Alexander McQueen* attire, scripture suggests that "Strength and honor are your clothing" (Proverbs 31:25). Life is about more than the *Christian Louboutin* heels, that you walk in. It's about the Christian life, that you choose to walk out each day. It's not about you wearing *St. John*, it's about you reading St. John. When you read the scripture in John 3:16, then you will understand the enormity of God's love for you. So much so, that He sent Jesus to die for you, so that you can live for Him. The agony and pain that He endured to love you, should empower you to love yourself and others.

When you remain prayed up, you clothe yourself with the whole armor of God, in order to slay the enemy and overcome adversity. Wake, pray, and slay each day.

Ephesians 6:14-17 tells us about the war clothes needed to slay the enemy. You must have your loins girt about with truth and wear the breastplate of righteousness. Your feet must be covered, with the preparation of the Gospel of peace. Take the shield of faith, the helmet of salvation, and the sword of the Spirit, which is God's Word.

You have all of this armor, but you don't have anything for

your back, because God doesn't expect you to run from the

enemy. You're armed and dangerous because "If you resist

the devil, he will flee from you" (James 4:7). Your enemy is

not your sister, it's the adversary who goes about as a

"Roaring lion seeking whom he may devour" (I Peter 5:8).

The devil desires to devour your dreams and relationships.

The enemy wants to steal, kill, and destroy your life. Your

faith will prevail beyond fear, because you possess the heart

of a fighter. The enemy or opposition doesn't stand a chance,

because you're armed and dangerous.

NEEDY OR NEEDED?

Dear Queen, any real man will tell you that there's nothing

more attractive than a beautiful, intelligent, sophisticated,

goal-oriented, kind hearted, and spiritual woman whose life

reflects love. A real man is not only concerned about the color and curves of a woman, he's impressed by the content of her character. The color that he's most interested in, is comprised of a heart of gold. The curve that's most endearing on your body, is the one that forms when you smile.

Be the virtuous woman of value, that God created you to be. Never be the type of woman that needs a man, be the type of woman that a man needs. Your presence should affirm that you're not needy, you're needed.

Begin to become the type of person that you're looking for, because you will attract the type of person that you are. You will attract what you're thinking. If your mindset is negative, begin to change your thinking and you will change what you're attracting. You can easily find someone in the club or a vixen, but a virtuous Queen is a rare jewel.

THE BEST FOR THE BEST

How can God send you the right one, if you're still connected to the wrong person? He will not release His best, if you're entangled in drama and mess. Don't settle for a momentary substitute, when God has the right attribute to fit you, for a lifetime. Your promise comes with a promotion. It's better to wait for the best, rather than settle for less.

Do you have the discipline to wait and go through the season(s), where God is the potter, you are the clay, and He molds you each day? When you're the clay, you feel the potter working on the intricate places of your life.

No, it's not comfortable but it's necessary. It doesn't feel good now, but it's going to work out for your good in the end. Trust Him through the process. Stop looking for someone to complete you, only God does that. He's not giving a half person, to a whole person. He wants you to be made whole. In order for that to happen, you have to trust

God and place the shattered pieces of your life, in His hands.

The situation that you went through, was only designed to bring out the best in you. When everyone else says the worst about you, God sees the best in you. None of us are perfect, but we can't give up in pursuit of perfection. Strive to be the best. God is saving the best, for the best. A Queen deserves a King, who will love and treat her the best.

GQ

By nature men are hunters. We are naturally competitive and seek a challenge. It's who we are and it's ingrained in our DNA. So it goes like this, if you run I chase, but if you chase I run. Queen, you will continually be out of breath and your feet will always be tired, if you're chasing a man. Stop chasing somebody, who doesn't want to be caught. He is alluding and avoiding you, because he's not interested in you. The truth hurts, but it will help you.

Like they say, "We adore those who ignore us and we ignore those who adore us." Oftentimes, a man pays attention to the woman, who is not paying attention to him. He's looking, but you're steadily focusing, on working and handling your business. Some men find that type of woman attractive.

Instead of being the person who is in somebody's face, take the time to invest in yourself and your career. Let a man find you, reaching for your goals and dreams, instead of his dollars.

A real King is *GQ*, not because of what he wears on the outside, but because of who he is on the inside. Yes, he is significant and successful. He smells and looks good. He's G'd up from the feet up. He dresses impeccably and speaks intelligently (let me stop bragging on myself). Queen, you know that he could easily be on the cover of *Gentlemen's Quarterly*, but more importantly he possesses a *Gentlemen's*

Quality from within.

Of all the attributes, the main and most important of all is that he has a relationship with God. The Genesis of a gentleman, emanates from his connection to Christ. He has an understanding of self, and the value that he brings to a relationship. Opening doors, kind acts of chivalry, communication, respecting, and treating a woman like a Queen is rooted in his character. A real King will pursue you like he's still trying to get you, even after he already has your heart. He's still interested in chasing you, just to ensure nothing will replace the love he has for you. A King seeks to protect his Queen's heart and love her through adversity.

A man is not a construction project, stop trying to fix him. If he doesn't want to treat you right or pay attention to you, then you can't convince him otherwise. Only God can change someone. Too often we walk into relationships and waste our time, trying to change people. If God hasn't changed them, then you surely can't change the person who

God made. Real men at work understand that to be under

construction, requires following God's instruction. He knows

that there is a King inside of him and walks as one in royalty.

PROVERBS 31

Proverbs 31:10 asks, "Who can find a virtuous woman? For

her price is far above rubies." In essence, if I can buy her,

then she is not the one. Notice, the scripture never asked,

"Who can find a voluptuous vixen?" It doesn't say, "Who

can find a pretty face and a slim waist?" Beauty is only skin

deep. It's fleeting and it fades. So you won't find that.

Rather, you will find a virtuous woman as the quality of

person required. In a world of quantity, a Queen knows her

value, worth, and quality.

Proverbs 20:6 also affirms, "Who can find a faithful

man?" For the writer to include that assertion, means there's little supply and great demand. Gospel singer, VaShawn Mitchell would say, "I've searched all over and couldn't find nobody. I looked high and low, still couldn't find nobody." Quantity is everywhere, but quality is rare.

Never go into a relationship, if you're not healed. You will always make bad choices, when you choose from weakness rather than strength. Don't choose somebody to change them. You can't change anybody, only God can do that. If they are not what you want, don't waste your time and energy, trying to make somebody become what you want them to be. If they are not what you want, then it's not your time and it's not the one. On the contrary, sometimes what you want is not what you need. It will never be the right time, if it's the wrong person. Don't rush into, what you will end up regretting. You never want to lower your standards, just for the sake of having somebody. A Queen deserves a King, not a Joker.

DUST SETTLES, I DON'T

Some of us have been so low, that all we settle for is the worst and only trust the dust. Shake yourself and get up. Stop discounting yourself, when you are priceless. When you see your value and know your worth, you will attract people who recognize what you see in yourself. Waiting for what you want, is better than settling for what you don't want. Queens don't chase. Queens are pursued by Kings. Don't chase somebody, who is running from you. Any person that you have to chase, is trying to get away.

If God sent it, you won't have to chase it. What is meant for you, won't run away from you. When you become a person of love, you will attract it. You won't have to chase it. Stop chasing and start preparing, for what you intend on attracting. You may have been through the worst, but you're still deserving of the best. Don't settle, your future is brighter than your past.

GET YOUR LIFE

I'm telling you like the singer Tamar Braxton, "Get your life!" Don't let your life slip away and fall into the hands, of somebody who doesn't know your worth. When you're going to the next level, you can't afford to settle. You're too special to just settle for anything, when God wants to give you the best of everything. When you become a person of love, you will attract love. You won't have to beg for it or chase it. Start preparing, for what you intend on attracting and receiving. Aspire to attain the best and settle for nothing less.

EXPRESSIONS FROM A KING

Dear Queen, I know you manage your time wisely, dress exquisitely, speak intelligently, smile beautifully, and cook deliciously (at least I hope). From your smile to what you say, the way you talk and that walk, when your hips sway. You've smiled, when you weren't happy. You dressed up, when things were messed up. They failed to applaud and appreciate you, for who you are and what you do. Yet you still push through.

At the end of the day, you just want a King who understands, what it means to have a Queen and the value that you bring. You realize that it's more than your beauty and makeup on the outside, but it's what you're made of that matters on the inside. The right one will hold you down, but not hold you back. He will see the best in you, in bad times. Prepare yourself for the right hands and heart that will love, appreciate, and celebrate your value. You know how to be everything to everybody, but the right one is coming to be your special somebody.

Dear Queen, I celebrate you because of the value that you bring. Nothing on God's green earth, can compare to your value and self-worth. Realize that you are a person of love and are too unique to compete for love. Never settle or you will get less than you deserve. You are the best and deserve the best. You are precious and priceless. You're too rare to give yourself to just anyone, when God has the perfect one for you.

What you want to last doesn't always happen fast. It's not delayed or denied, it will happen at the right time. While God is preparing you for the right one, He's preparing the right one for you. The right man will cherish, love, and invest in you. For what it's worth, he knows your worth. He will recognize your value, rather than diminish you. A good woman like you is deserving of a good man, who will love, respect, and protect your heart in his hand.

Dear Queen, your King wants to change two things about you…your last name and address. He's impressed by your heart, not just your hips. The most important curve, is the smile that forms on your lips.

This time, the tears that flow down your face will

come from the joy of your future, to wash away the pain of the past. The tears will replace, the years of hurt in your heart. Your King will not come to take, but to give greater love to you and reveal the best in you.

The right man knows your worth and will invest in you, to uplift and empower you. The right investment won't leave you emotionally bankrupt, with a broken heart. Be patient and pursue your purpose. God's timing is better than yours. Don't rush it or you will ruin it. While you're trusting and waiting, keep working to invest in yourself. The right one will be an asset, not a liability. They will be your teammate, not an opponent.

All of the opponents you faced, were simply preparing you for the right teammate that God will place in your life. A King and Queen won't fight each other. They will fight for each other. Real Kings and Queens, encourage, uplift, support, and pray for each other. You're a team that can rise above anything, when you stand together on everything.

ALL HAIL THE QUEEN

Dear Queen, you earn respect from Kings like me, because your beauty goes beyond your body and is shaped by your mentality. You're not the type, to just give yourself to anybody. You know that your value and inner beauty, is not for everybody. Those who didn't appreciate you, made you value yourself more.

To approach a Queen means, you have to bring more to the table than an appetite. A woman who knows her worth, knows that she's more than her breast, legs, hips, and thighs...that pop eyes. Look past her assets and realize, she is an asset. She's a Queen that can empower a King, one whose worthy of a ring.

A Queen who knows what she brings to the table, doesn't mind eating alone. A Queen would rather be in the company, of someone who sees her value, than a person whose only blind to it. Don't pass up your blessing. She brings favor to the table. If you're blind, the next man will see what you weren't able.

It's one thing to be stimulated by the physical. It's another thing to be sharpened intellectually, emotionally, and spiritually which produces longevity. A Queen doesn't compete with her King, she collaborates with him. She's not solely focused on his money, but his mentality. Not what he drives, but what drives him. From his tie, to his time she becomes the spring in his step and shapes the point, that sharpens him. A King can tell his Queen, "I'm a movement by myself, but I'm a force when we're together."

Dear Queen, you see in a King, what the world often fails to recognize. You stand by us in good times and have our back in trying times. Your words of encouragement and tender pat on the back, propels us forward into our purpose.

A real Queen, knows how to speak to the King in you. A real King has love in his heart, a vision in his mind, and strength in his back to lift his Queen to higher heights. When a King has love from his Queen, he can stand up to anything.

A Queen who wants best for you, is best for you. She's blind to what you used to be and only sees what you will become. She not only sees with her eyes, but with her heart. She's the type of woman, you can't drag your feet with or sleep on. Play around if you want to, you'll wake up and be alarmed. A King decided to put a Queen on his arm. As she's a blessing to you, she will be the best thing that ever happened to you. She sees the best in you and wants the best for you.

Dear Queen when life pushes you down, your King will lift you up. The right one is praying for you, because they see the best in you and want the best for you. You don't need a person who is only there in good times, but disappears

DEAR QUEEN - DR. EDDIE CONNOR

in bad times. If you have a warm heart of love, it doesn't matter how cold it gets. Through sunshine and stormy seasons, a love that's built to last will stand the tests of time. Real love makes it feel like summer, in the cold of winter. You endured the storms, rain, and fires of adversity. All the while, God was preparing you for the right one and He was preparing the right one for you. Remain focused and ready to receive, what God wants you to have.

ROYALTY DEMANDS LOYALTY

Dear Queen, you have to love you before you expect someone else to. As you become a person of love, you will become a magnet for love. When your heart is in God's hands, He will give it to the right man who knows how to love, provide, and protect you. Love yourself and know your worth in a greater way, each day. You are worth waiting for and your love is worth looking for.

The right one for you understands that love is a verb, expressed through action. Your King is a man of his word, who studies God's Word. Real relationships have reciprocity. It's giving and receiving from both levels, that goes beyond ego. It's solely focused on how "we grow." Keep working your purpose while you pray and prepare, for the proposal from a King that's loyal. A real man knows a woman's worth and realizes, a love like yours is royal.

Know that your price is far above rubies and your royalty demands loyalty. While they're partying, keep preparing. Queen take pride in knowing, that God has a King who will not only give you a ring, but be your lifetime blessing. Your King will forever stand by your side, support, and embrace you as love abides. Real love doesn't hurt you, it heals, empowers, and sustains you.

THE QUEEN OF HEARTS

In his book *Alice's Adventures in Wonderland*, Lewis Carroll describes the character, *The Queen of Hearts* as a foul-mouthed monarch, mixed with rage and a blind fury. She gives death sentences and famously exclaims, "Off with their heads" for the slightest offense. Her attitude feels like the cold of winter, in the heat of summer. You would think a character named *The Queen of Hearts* would have love flowing from her heart. Unfortunately, bitterness, rage, hurt, and animosity is at the root of her heart. As I peered through the looking glass, I wondered why *The Queen of Hearts* was angry? What was the source of her attitude and animosity? One instance points to the fact, that she saw Alice and the cards painting white roses red.

Oftentimes, people are upset because you decided to grab the paintbrush of purpose and add color to your life. Their life remains bland, while yours becomes bold. Haters with no heart become upset, because you transformed a thorny situation, into something beautiful. Your thorns brought you closer to God's throne.

Rather than learn from Alice and the cards, the Queen threatened to kill them. Keep in mind that *The Queen of Hearts* is an adult, but Alice is only a child. From the time you were a child the enemy has tried to kill you. From the days of your youth, people have hurt you and tried to destroy your life. They have tried to steal your innocence. Family members and so called friends, who were supposed to support you, attempted to kill your dreams. They threatened to kill you, because they didn't want you to birth the purpose within. They didn't realize that you were a rose, handcrafted by God and designed to shine. You were born to bloom and breakthrough.

TAKE ME TO THE KING

If it wasn't for the King, Alice would have been killed. You need to understand, that if it wasn't for the King of Kings, you would have died a long time ago. The enemy would have destroyed your dreams and murdered your mission, if the King didn't rescue you. When life tears you apart, only the King of Kings can restore your heart.

Oftentimes, life makes you the Queen of broken hearts. If you have not healed your heart, it will cause you to break anyone's heart that comes across your path. You will play games with men, because someone played games with you. The wrong joker hurt your heart and it ripped your life apart. In the end you play yourself, because you will always lose at your own game. Nothing is worse than being a brokenhearted Queen. The King of Kings will remedy the source of hurt, when you seek to reveal and identify it. No matter how bad it made you feel.

Much like *The Queen of Hearts*, you internalize rage. Someone mistreated you and now you're mean, angry, and refuse to let anyone get close to your heart. When you're pleased, you can be pleasant. However, you're still bossy and often remain impatient, to where your attitude can change to rage. In the words of Bruno Mars, "Throw some perm on your attitude. Girl you gotta relax."

You have connected to so many jokers, that you can't even recognize a King. The pain has skewed your vision. Through it all, God is healing you, to release a loving spirit in you. His love will cause you to be the true Queen of Hearts. Your love within, will overcome hate and your purpose will outweigh the pain. Real love will flow from your heart, to bring hope and healing to the lives you touch.

DAUGHTER OF DESTINY

God is your Heavenly Father and you are his daughter of destiny. Any real father, wants his daughter to be the best and have the best. God is no different. He gave his SON to erase the darkness of your past and bring the SUN into your life, to shine for the rest of your life. He wants his daughter of destiny, to have the best son of substance that will love and empower you.

No relationship is perfect. We all have baggage. The right one will help you to unpack it, discard of it, detach from it, and break out of the box. It doesn't matter how good you look on the outside, we all have some issues on the inside. The right one, will look past your past and see your heart. They will see who you're becoming, not what you've been. Don't take old baggage, into a new relationship. A new relationship won't heal you, until you deal with the old one that hurt you. Let the pain of the past go, so you can love like you've never been hurt before. Shake off what is weighing you down, in order to soar to new heights.

It takes the right tools to build it, with the right one who will support it. A King and Queen work to build each other up, not break each other down. They lift one another up, not pull each other down. The right one will be there with a shoulder to lean on, hands to help, arms to embrace, and a heart to love.

Getting married won't heal you and being single, won't kill you. Be content in whatever state you are in. Wait on God or the weight of rushing, will hurt you in the long run. It's better to wait for the right one, than settle for just someone right now. Being alone doesn't mean you're lonely. It just means you're getting ready.

What you're getting ready to gain, is better than what you lost. Don't lose your mind over the person in your past, because you're going to need your mind for the person in your future. Trust and believe that what's ahead, is far greater than what you left behind. The dream you're about to receive, is greater than the nightmare you released.

GOD BLESS THE KING AND QUEEN

A love like yours, can't be found on every corner or block.
God bless the King, who has the key to your heart. You can
be sure that your heart is protected and your relationship is
secure, when it's in God's hands.

A complete relationship includes three (God, you, and
them) which brings greater unity. Prepare for what you're
praying to receive. The right man will lead you. He will do
more than PAY for you. He will PRAY with and for you.
Don't stress over it, put it in God's hands and let Him handle
it. Just plan, prepare, and pray. God will work it out, if you
don't get in His way.

Dear Queen, a man with a plan will point you in the
direction of your purpose. A King is a servant in God's
Kingdom. A King knows how to lead you, because he
follows God. He sees greatness in you, because has a vision
for you.

A King will transform his vision into action. On the road to destiny, don't get distracted. Your future is brighter than your past. Open your eyes to see, that where you're going is far greater than where you've been.

Your direction is in your connection. The right connection comes with a plan, vision, and action. Keep your eyes to the future and your back to the past. Your king will point you in the direction of your dreams. Prepare now for what will come to pass and what is intended to last.

Dear Queen, your King will only have eyes for you. None will compare to the beauty in you. True beauty goes beyond your curves on the outside, it speaks to your character on the inside. The cute curve from the smile he places on your face, will illuminate any place. The right person, will not only see you with their eyes, but they will envision your greatness from their heart. The wrong one was blind to your value, but the right one will see your virtue.

Queen, place your heart in God's hands and he will put it in a King's hand. Too many people, have extended their hands to take. The right one, will use theirs to give. They won't hit or hurt you. They will heal and help you. Your King will love, protect, and provide for you. For all your pain through the years, get ready to experience true tears of joy.

A King and Queen will always be secure, in each other's hands because their trust is in God's hands. A king will open your door, your mind, and your heart. His words will be followed through, by his actions. He will be good to you and for you. He will be an asset not a liability, strength and compatibility.

THERE'S A QUEEN IN YOU

There is a Queen inside of you, to challenge the systems of society. There is a Queen in you, that will expand the parameters of your mind and the minds of others. There is a Queen in you, that will dream and not only dream, but take action. There is a Queen in you, that will empower communities and expose youth to opportunities. There is a Queen in you that has compassion for the least of these, those who are impoverished and disadvantaged.

There is a Queen in you, that will invent, invest, and imbibe power into the lives of others. We must dream, strive, and succeed together. We must do it so well, that the living, dead, or unborn couldn't do it any better.

Dear Queen, as Dr. King declared, "If you can't fly then run, if you can't run then walk, if you can't walk then crawl, but whatever you do you have to keep moving forward." Whatever you do keep moving forward, maximize every moment, and live through dying places. Transform every hurt into healing, think positive in negative situations, and keep your mind on your mission. For all of your adversity, God is giving you a crown of glory. You will receive an incorruptible crown of life and righteousness. Rejoice because God is giving you beauty for ashes.

My *Dear Queen* it's time to breakthrough. Greatness is in you and upon you, for there is a Queen in you. Mount up on wings as eagles. So soar into the stratosphere of success, like Mae Jamison. Be a Queen, like Coretta Scott King. When they go low, you go high like Michelle Obama. Represent for the people, like Barbara Jordan. Rise to new heights, like Dorothy Height. Turn pain into poetry, like Maya Angelou. Demand R-E-S-P-E-C-T, like Aretha Franklin. Get active and demand equal rights, like Fannie Lou Hamer. You're a modern day Rosa Parks, Betty Shabazz, Madam C.J. Walker, Sister Souljah, Sojourner Truth, Dorothy Dandridge, Althea Gibson, Harriet Tubman, and Shirley Chisholm. You come from Kings and Queens. Be the rose that grows through concrete. Bloom where you're planted. Impact locally. Influence globally.

CROWN OF GLORY

Much like Queen Esther of the Bible, you may have been exiled into anonymity but your wisdom will bring you into the land of opportunity. Wear your crown because you were created to be a Queen, for such a time as this (Esther 4:14). God has the final say and you will receive a crown of glory, that will never fade away (I Peter 5:4). Don't wait for people to recognize your royalty. Crown yourself. Crown yourself with love. Crown yourself with greatness. Crown yourself with righteousness. Crown yourself with power and peace.

Isaiah 62:3 declares, "You shall be a crown of glory, in the hand of the Lord." There is a Queen in you, because the King of Kings gave His life for you. Live with purpose, on purpose, and for a purpose to inspire the world. You are your sister's keeper. Don't breakdown, breakthrough. Make no apologies for being amazing. Wear your crown. Smile and let your beauty shine through. There's a Queen in you!

THE QUEEN CODE

Real Queens love God.
Real Queens love themselves and others.
Real Queens pray.
Real Queens nurture their children and family.
Real Queens are strong wives and mothers.
Real Queens are committed.
Real Queens display care, character,
commitment, and concern.
Real Queens keep their word.
Real Queens keep it real.
Real Queens uplift their community.
Real Queens bring unity.
Real Queens recognize the Queen within themselves.
Real Queens strengthen their sisters.
Real Queens empower their brothers.
Real Queens mentor others.
Real Queens show respect.
Real Queens respect themselves.
Real Queens read.
Real Queens lead.
Real Queens are genuine.
Real Queens are unique.
Real Queens don't compete.
Real Queens have a vision.
Real Queens are dedicated.
Real Queens are educated.
Real Queens are intellectual.
Real Queens are successful.
Real Queens build their Queendom.
Real Queens wear their crown.
Real Queens lift you up, when you are down.

Real Queens serve.
Real Queens transform struggles into strengths.
Real Queens are righteous.
Real Queens are virtuous.
Real Queens are their sister's keeper.
Real Queens are not perfect, but they strive
to perfect their lives each day.

Real men understand that a **QUEEN**,
speaks to the King in you.
She nurtures, encourages, upgrades, and inspires you.

Her beauty resides not only on the OUTSIDE,
it shines from the INSIDE.
She knows her worth, being priceless from birth.

A **QUEEN** is more than her ASSETS,
she is an ASSET.
Look into the mirror of your soul,
there is strength to press toward your goal.

There is no need to COMPETE, for a **QUEEN** is
COMPLETE. So she COMPLEMENTS her
COMPANION, to form a more perfect union.

In a world of QUANTITY,
you are a **QUEEN** of QUALITY!

Quintessentially
Unique
Empowering
Everyone
Naturally

Dear Queen

QUEEN you are…Quintessentially Unique
Empowering Everyone Naturally.
Look into the mirror of your soul,
your beauty I behold.
Understand and know your worth.
More splendid than creation,
on God's green earth.
You're pregnant with purpose, promise,
possibility, and potential.
It's time to give birth to the real you,
avoid the superficial.
Let your hair down,
free your mind and unwind.
You're more intoxicating,
than Moscato or Merlot.
When beauty is only skin deep,
it's love inside that helps you grow.
When life makes others uptight,
you remain mellow.
I can see the gold in you,
through your 50 shades
of gorgeous beautiful sun kissed skin.
It's the favor on you and elegant
grace that helps you win.
It's not about what you drive,
but what drives you within.
There's something in you,
that attracts me to you.
I see greatness in you.
When others only stop,
to stare at your behind.

I search deeper, being attracted
to the vision in your mind.
Your desires and dreams take you
to another altitude,
because you have the right attitude.
Your goals and standards,
are higher than your heels.
Your wisdom spans, beyond your years.
Nations will rise and call you blessed,
because you're gifted to be the best.
Understand you're more than your assets,
because you are an asset.
Your greatest curve supersedes
your effervescent pulchritude.
It's your crooked smile that lights the world,
because the SON shines through you.
No one can dim your light,
because of the bright future in front of you.
Take my hand, we all have a past
but our future can outlast it too.
Repair fractured dreams and broken promises.
The pains, the hurts,
our flaws and scars are obvious.
Never to hurt or harm you,
only here to heal and help you.
A heart bright enough,
to light a thousand worlds.
Warm enough, to heat arctic winters.
Makes the world feel like July in December.
Let me lead and guide you,
to unveil the Queen that's inside you.
If a majestic purple Prince from Minneapolis
could give you diamonds and pearls,

it would never compare
to the unique royal virtue
rooted deep within you girl.
Love is the GPS that provides the route to your heart.
Like a trees roots, intertwined like
an embrace felt
and hands held when hearts collide.
You're a Queen who exudes quality
and that's what you're focused on, not quantity.
Look at how the Creator,
fearfully and wonderfully made you.
Picasso, Basquiat, Michelangelo,
Rembrandt, or Warhol could never do.
Good God beauty, just oozing out of you.
Coated in caramel, lightly sprinkled
with a hazel hue.
Mentally, spiritually, and physically framed
to where you drive brothers insane.
Makes them lose their mind,
when they can't get your number
or even your name.
I don't know who you are,
but I need to know who you are.
Make no apologies, because it's no surprise
that you're seen as a prize.
Those other guys are only fixated
on your breast, legs, and thighs
as if you're fast food to just pop eyes.
Yes, Popeyes.
Just the way you are, is by far incredible.
You're too unique to compete.
The mark you leave is indelible.
You're not the type of woman that needs a man.

You're the type that a man needs.
You meet his needs with real love, commitment,
dedication and honesty.
Honestly, I don't need you to be Beyoncé,
Gabrielle Union, Halle Berry, or Marilyn Monroe.
Just be who God made you.
Let your inner beauty glow.
For what God has placed in you,
is greater than any hurt or hate
that seeks to replace the love in you.
Your royal radiance, can unlock
the King in me, Queen.
Take my hand,
let's soar on eagles wings.
Building castles of love
as Stevie wonder sings…
Quintessentially Unique
Empowering Everyone Naturally.
YOU are my ***DEAR QUEEN.***

ACKNOWLEDGMENTS

My sincerest appreciation is extended to the following individuals, in gratitude for their contribution and support. My Mama Dr. Janice Connor, Elijah Connor, The Norbrook Publishing Team, Don Smith, Jay Melton, Madeline Melton, Hawk, Vincina Person, Royda Urey, Tonya Cross, Marjani Jackson, Trabian Shorters, Bishop James Winslow, Christina Johnson, Principal Lisa Phillips, Dr. Ken, and Dr. Vivian Johnson. To all of the students and staff at Cody High School and Cass Tech High School. Thank you for allowing me to empower our young people, to lead and succeed. God bless every Queen, who reads this book and wears their crown.

Much love,

Dr. Eddie

ABOUT THE AUTHOR

Dr. Eddie Connor is a bestselling author, college professor, international speaker, and radio/TV correspondent. He is a survivor of stage four cancer and empowers people to overcome obstacles. As a writer of seven books, he is the cousin of one of the world's most influential entertainers and musicians, Prince.

Dr. Eddie is the CEO of the literacy organization, *Boys 2 Books*, which provides mentorship to young males via literacy, leadership, and life skills enrichment. As an assistant to Rep. Hansen Clarke, their Congressional resolution became the impetus for President Barack Obama's national *My Brother's Keeper* initiative.

He has been featured and hosted segments on CBS, FOX News, NBC, PBS, The Steve Harvey TV Show, The Tom Joyner Show, and The Word Network. He was also featured in the acclaimed BET documentary, *It Takes a Village to Raise Detroit.*

Dr. Eddie is a 2016 recipient of *The President's Volunteer Service Award* from The White House. He speaks extensively on the subjects of education, healthy relationships, leadership, overcoming obstacles, and maximizing your purpose. He empowers people at churches, conferences, community centers, and colleges, by inspiring and motivating others to overcome the odds.

Dr. Eddie grew up in Kingston, Jamaica and is a proud resident of Detroit, Michigan.

CONNECT WITH DR. EDDIE

To request Dr. Eddie for speaking engagements, media interviews, or for bulk book purchases, please email: **info@EddieConnor.com**

WEBSITE:
www.EddieConnor.com

SOCIAL MEDIA:
Facebook.com/EddieConnorJr
Instagram.com/EddieConnorJr
Twitter.com/EddieConnorJr
Snapchat: EddieConnorJr
Youtube.com/EddieConnor
#DearQueen

Made in the USA
Lexington, KY
30 March 2017